DEAR BROTHERS AND SISTERS

Gender and Its Responsibility

Elder George

PublishAmerica
Baltimore

ISBN: 1-4241-6391-9
PUBLISHED BY PUBLISHAMERICA, LLLP
www.publishamerica.com
Baltimore

Printed in the United States of America

To My Brothers and Sisters

May the contents of this book shed light on your gender attributes and the contributions they enable you to make to the universal family.

Contents

Preface

Since my late youth I sensed a societal tension, which I could not clearly define, but the symptoms of which were becoming increasingly apparent. I noticed that the spirit of comradery among men was declining, that the media was taking an increasingly adversarial position between men and women, and that the relationship between women and women was becoming increasingly superficial. These trends were symptomatic of a weakening tribal and family structure, which was resulting in a growing disrespect for all forms of authority.

This disrespect for authority took many forms. People no longer "dressed up" as a measure of respect when visiting elders or institutions. The term Mr. or Mrs. was dropped and the first name was used in all forms of address. Professional athletes discontinued allegiance to teams, and became free agents. Corporate loyalty gave way to individual gain, and job changes increased. The police were no longer held in high esteem, universities were burned, and Presidents from both political parties were in disrepute. Disco dancing replaced ballroom dancing as an expression of women being independent of the leadership of men. The elders left the tribe and went to live in retirement communities, wives sought out-of-the-home employment and independent careers, the rate of divorce increased, and children were put in nursery schools.

Traditional activities no longer seemed to work. The family that prayed together did not necessarily stay together. Church-going children O.D. on drugs as did non-church-going children. The clergy could not hold families together because their own families were disintegrating. A priest would run off with a married woman. a minister would run off with the organist—and the organist was a man, and the rabbi would have a Buddhist mistress. Psychiatrists, psychologists, and therapists were also having an increasing incidence of divorce, as were all professional people.

All types of standards were deteriorating and disappearing. Morality and ethics were so diluted as to be nonexistent. What used to be gutter language became modern syntax. A man's word being his bond gave way to the phrase "so I lied" and it was used on programming of every major network. Having a hooker visit one's home was also a requirement on all TV programs, and they all seemed to being doing quite well in their professions, a point that was not missed by young impressionable girls watching these shows. Adultery, incest, pornography, and general licentiousness became standard fare on home television. The First Amendment was used as a vehicle to reduce the influence of the teachings of the Torah, Bible, Koran, Tao, Upanishads, of Confucius and the Buddha. Dishonesty became a norm in societal relations.

The schoolmarm of the one room schoolhouse had given our children a better education than the high tech school environments that were developing. The manner in which education was handled became symbolic of society's solution to all problems: just throw money at it. The more we spent on education, the less our children were learning. The more we spent on society, the more the fabric of society seemed to be unraveling. Yet the idea that money was the solution to all ills became pervasive, bringing about the worst practice of democratic government—the election of government officials on the basis of how much government money they could bring into their locale. Everyone was on the take. Spend, spend, spend was the requirement of government office. People were not worried about the budget or fiscal policy; they just wanted more of everything.

The disappearance of standards resulted in a doing "one's thing" philosophy, which evolved into narcissism. All self-help activities, whether religious, spiritual, mental, physical, emotional, or psychological, were imbued with the glorification of self, rather than the motivation to serve others. Religious doctrine became bastardized and the legitimacy and authenticity of spiritual teachings became suspect. Bacchanalian lifestyles flourished as the thirst for pleasure became insatiable. Drug usage of all sorts became de rigueur.

We were the richest nation in the world, yet poverty was spreading. We were the freest nation in the world, yet we could not build prisons fast enough to house all the convicts. We were the most religiously oriented industrial nation, yet immorality was rampant.

Something fundamental was obviously wrong, but what? I wrote letters to TV program directors, editors, and various organizations, calling for the need to restore family values. Yet I myself became a victim or a participant in the general deterioration of societal structure and values, having gone through a divorce and seen my family disperse. What was happening in and to America? What? What? What?

I noticed that creativity, or at least the results of creative, and especially conceptual thinking, were on a severe decline. Every conceptual invention that was within the common knowledge of society occurred in the first half of the century. The automobile, airplane, phonograph, motion picture projector, radio, television, rocketry, atomic power, radar, sonar, computer, and even the transistor, were all invented before 1950. With the tremendous increase in college education and scientific knowledge in the last half of the twentieth century, why was conceptual thinking on the decline?

With the hundreds of billions of dollars spent on the Great Society, why was poverty on the increase? Why, concurrent with the Great Society, were men being put into cages at an ever-increasing rate?

Why, with the great emphasis on relationships, in schools, on TV, radio, the printed media, new age philosophy, and in self help organizations, were there fewer marriages, more rapes, more sexual harassment, and a general inability to make commitments? Why have the values of women changed, from wanting to be desired not only for their bodies, but for their hearts and minds as well; to giving only their bodies but not their hearts and minds? Why do they, on a subconscious level, increasingly seek out those men who won't make commitments? Why were men being called stupid for having large families, when there was a time that they were admired for doing so? Why did husbands and wives stop being understanding of each other's weaknesses and idiosyncrasies? Why, with the new emphasis on relationships were we told, "don't put up with him" or "don't put up with her"? The more we were talking about relationships, the less we were having them. Yet people were just as good as they ever were. The world was still on its upward path of spiritual evolvement. Why weren't we getting along?

Why had we run away from all the institutions that normally provide people comfort? I can remember in my youth the warmth and security that emanated from all tribal structures. The women visiting in the kitchen discussing the issues which were important to them, and the men visiting in the living room discussing the issues that were important to them. Life was full of tribal activities: weddings, funerals, baptisms, bar mitzvahs, and confirmations. If one of the men of the tribe was not treating his wife properly, the other men would pay him a visit and tell him how the men of their tribe take care of their women, and he would usually alter his behavior. If a woman was not treating her husband properly, some old grandmother would pay her a visit and explain how the women of the tribe treat their men, and she would usually adjust her behavior. There was always some old auntie somewhere who was doing her part to hold the tribe together, to introduce single people to each other, to give advice and consolation.

The clergy were usually part of tribal activities, and the minister, priest and rabbi were invited to most of the important familial and tribal functions. Even the local doctor and schoolteacher were invited to these functions, for they took care of and educated the tribe. If there was a secure nest, the tribal structure was it. If there was safety, a sense of belonging, knowing that you were cared for, it was in the presence of the tribe. Yet, most tribal structures have disappeared with hardly a vestige remaining.

These tribal structures were based on ethnicity, religion, and race, and as intermarriage between various ethnic, racial and religious groups increased, society became more homogeneous, and the clearly defined lines of these cultures began to blur, fade, and eventually disappear. This was natural. What was unnatural was the lack of development of new tribal cultures to replace the old, and I realized that herein was the major cause of the societal problems that were developing. However, while I did realize that new tribal structures were not forming, I did not know the reason, nor did I fully comprehend the effect that the lack of these tribal structures was having on the nation.

I did notice that the relationship between men and women was becoming strained. This was a puzzling experience for me, as I had an excellent social life with the opposite sex that began in grade school, and consisted of going to house parties, dances, roller skating, beach parties, church and school events, the movies, night clubs, and a multitude of other activities. Ever since my teen years, the opposite sex had confided in me, whether friends, acquaintances, or complete strangers whom I would meet on the train, bus, subway, plane, in hotels, and at business conventions. They would sit next to me and voluntarily share the most intimate details of their lives. I learned a lot about women in this manner, and not a small amount of the information contained in this book came from these experiences. Nevertheless, I too, began to feel a strained relationship with women. This occurred not in the social realm, but in the functional realm of society.

I noticed that at business meetings, PTA meetings, church council meetings, and other societal functions, I was not comfortable with the increased involvement of women. Apparently many men weren't either, for articles were written that when women learned a particular function that had been in the domain of men, the men would stop participating in that function. When women started ushering in church, fewer men volunteered to usher. When women started appearing on the church council, it became more difficult to find men to volunteer for the council. This was occurring in all sorts of organizations and even in universities that had gone from single sex education to coeducation. What was the reason for this phenomenon?

I felt that the passing of the tribal structure and the discomfort and antagonisms developing between the sexes were related, but I wasn't sure how. I did realize that men and women saw life differently, thought differently, and acted differently, but I could not clearly define these differences, nor could I determine to what degree they affected the functional realm of our activities. Like many people, I knew something was wrong, I also knew that somehow it was related to our difference in Gender, and that this difference had to be acknowledged and recognized.

Sitting in my living room one day and reflecting on all of the foregoing, I prayed for guidance in finding a cause and solution to these issues that seriously affected all of us. Shortly thereafter I came upon a book entitled "The Kybalion" which contained the teachings of Hermes Trismegistus, one of the earliest influences on philosophical and spiritual thinking. In reviewing the index of The Kybalion, I noticed one chapter entitled Gender, and another, Mental Gender. Here at last was the missing link of information that I needed to finally put the bow on the string around my package of causes, effects, and solutions, to the issues affecting society. I felt like a modern day Archimedes, who after learning that a floating body displaced its weight in water, ran through the streets of Athens shouting "Eureka," which means, I have found it!

I sure felt as though I had found it, for in the Kybalion the principle of Gender was defined. It was more than just a difference between the sexes, it was a principle that explained the operation of the entire universe, and of human society as well. After reading the

Kybalion, I reviewed various religious texts, and saw in all of them the underlying principle of Gender. I also observed that all the activities of modern society were Gender influenced, whether government, the economy, education, or religion.

I have explained in this book through a compilation of essays, the issues affecting us today as they relate to the universal principle of Gender, and the appropriate action to be taken to resolve these issues.

If you agree with what is written herein, then we can individually and collectively work to bring about the changes that will once again bring stability and relative harmony to our society, and enable us to more readily pursue the spiritual growth that is the purpose of our earthly existence.

I send my love to all of you.

I
Dear Brothers
And Sisters

Dear Brothers and Sisters,

Please think of this book as a letter, addressing an influence which began early in the 20th century, and that has caused many changes in our lives.

Each era had issues needing resolution in order for society to keep on its forward evolutionary path, and we too have issues that need resolving. The issue unique to our era is that the importance of Gender has been obscured as a result of our involvement in the industrial and postindustrial economy. We are serving the means of production, rather than having it serve us. This serving of the economy has altered our relationships to one another, to God, and to institutions, and has caused chaos and dissidence in our society.

We all know that the hammer is a tool, and that after we have finished hammering nails into a board, we put the hammer back in the toolbox, where it has no influence over us. We are the masters, and the hammer is our servant. This has also been true of our relationship to the plow over the centuries. It was used to till the fields in order to obtain the product used to nurture the race. We did not serve the plow; it served us.

As long as we knew that we were masters of the plow, we had a better perspective of our relationship to God and to one another. We knew that we were spiritual beings residing in material bodies. We knew that in our present stage of development we could only grow spiritually in these material bodies, and therefore the highest material calling was the propagation and preservation of the race. The proper balance of Gender, which is the basis of all existence, and which we knew to exist subjectively, and which was part of our inherent natures, accomplished this. The natural means of providing goods and services necessary for the propagation and preservation of the race has latterly been defined as Capitalism.

The above are the basic tenets of the viewpoint that will be expounded upon in this book. Our departure from these tenets is the underlying cause of the issues that are troubling society, such as the breakdown of the familial and tribal order, which has created a void that the State continually tries to fill. The laws, customs and traditions created for the well-being of the race have come into disrepute, and religious doctrine has become bastardized. Crime, rape, lying, cheating, adultery, unwed motherhood, venereal disease, and child abuse have all increased. The life expectancy of women in relation to that of men has decreased because of various forms of substance abuse. Academic standards and performance have deteriorated, as have reportorial standards in all media, and ethical standards in all professions. Respect has declined for all authority be it persons or institutions. We have the highest incarceration rate in the world and the highest murder rate of any industrial nation.

The State has taken over more and more of the natural masculine role in the family, setting standards for morality (actually removing them), child rearing, the care of the aged, and family income distribution. The more the State has replaced the masculine role, the more chaos has spread. The State is enacting laws that emasculate men in the economic arena similar to that done to men in the home, resulting in a decrease in daring, the pioneering spirit, and creativity, with the resultant stagnation of the economy.

Societal stability and economic growth can only be achieved by the return to a natural Gender based society. When the creative Will and pioneering spirit of the masculine Gender is combined with the nurturing loving manifestation of the feminine Gender, the race will most readily propagate and preserve itself on its journey toward spiritual growth.

Rather than attempt to "prove" these assertions by a critical and objective presentation of supporting data, as is the norm with most authors in our Western, scientifically-oriented society, I am instead using the approach of expressing my own views regarding the interpretation of data, as was used by Plato, Kant, Marx and others. Some of my assertions may prove to be erroneous, but others who believe in my basic philosophy will come to the fore and supply the necessary "proof", and will also push forward the knowledge of this particular subject. Also, we believe in our perceptions, not in proofs. John Keats wrote in a letter to a friend "nothing in this world is provable", and Emile Chartier said, "We prove what we want to prove". Let the test of the assertions made in this letter be "does it sound true to me", if it does, then it is true for you. If it doesn't sound true to you, then it isn't. All true knowledge is subjective. We just use our objectivity to gather information to support the subjective beliefs that we already have. Having said all this, it is my hope that the contents of this letter will "ring true" to you.

My hope is not only that the information contained in this book will "ring true" to you, but that you will "feel" it. That it will cause you to have a wide range of emotions, and that you will do something to bring forth change. The time for action is nearing. How much longer can we stand by and let the race deteriorate? How much longer can we stand by and watch our brothers and sisters suffer? I hope that your answer will be "not any longer", and that your actions will confirm your words.

A statement of the principles governing my assertions will be repeated throughout this book and are as follows:

1. Humankind is spirit in a material body—all else is religious theory.

2. The highest material purpose is the propagation and preservation of the race—all else is anthropological theory.

3. The manner in which humankind's spiritual and material objectives are attained is dependent upon the balance of Gender—all else is sociological theory.

4. Capitalism is the natural distribution of goods and services—all else is economic theory.

I thank you for having started to read this book, and hope that its contents will sufficiently interest you so that you will continue reading until the end, whereupon you will be motivated to partake in a movement that will bring about the betterment of the human race.

II
Basic Characteristics
of Gender

This chapter identifies the basic attributes of Gender. References to Gender attributes began with the ancients, and are found in the earliest religious and mystical teachings, and in various cultures, sciences and arts. For new-age-knowledge enthusiasts, numerology and astrology both contain references to Gender.

The forces of Gender act throughout the universe, and the universe itself cannot exist without the influence of Gender.

The creating, producing and generating of manifestations on every plane of existence, is the result of Gender.

As there is an anode and cathode in an electric storage battery, the attraction to each other causing the flow of electricity, there is also an anode and cathode influence in all life.

The cathode is the feminine - mother principle of electrical phenomena and of life. The feminine - mother principle is the one doing the productive and creative work.

The anode is the masculine - father principle, which is that of WILL, the directing and willing of energy towards the feminine principle, enabling it to create.

This union of the masculine and feminine principles is evident in the procreation of the race. The masculine principle of WILL becomes imbued in the nurturing feminine principle, enabling it to do its creative work, the creation of a child.

In the mental realm, the masculine principle is the objective, conscious and voluntary mind. The feminine principle is the subjective, subconscious, involuntary passive mind.

The "I" represents the masculine principle of Gender. It contains the Will that motivates the "ME".

The "ME" represents the feminine principle of Gender. It contains the thoughts, feelings and the emotions of the self, that require the direction of the "I" in order to produce and accomplish.

The tendency of the feminine principle is to receive impressions.

The tendency of the masculine principle is to give out, to express, to make impressions.

In order to better understand the effects of Gender influence on government, economics and society in general, it is best to first consider the positive and negative manifestations of each Gender.

THE POSITIVE MANIFESTATIONS OF THE MASCULINE GENDER ARE: individuality, originality, creativity, ambition, courage, independence, discipline, progressiveness, positiveness, self-sufficiency, leadership, daring, activeness, force, will-power, stability, constancy, pioneering spirit, abstract thinking, conditional love, contemplation.

THE NEGATIVE MANIFESTATIONS OF MASCULINE GENDER ARE: selfishness, laziness, insensitivity, stubbornness, imitation, dependency.

The extremes of the masculine Gender are: brutality and tyranny.

THE POSITIVE MANIFESTATIONS OF THE FEMININE GENDER ARE: cooperation, diplomacy, companionship, gentility, consideration, unconditional love, harmony, friendliness, rhythm, receptivity, nurturing, caring, giving, industriousness, materialism, visual thinking, accommodation.

THE NEGATIVE MANIFESTATIONS OF FEMININE GENDER ARE: vacillation, apathy, indifference, deceitfulness, carelessness, disloyalty, spinelessness.

The extremes of the feminine Gender are: cruelty, deception and chaos.

Every human being has within them the attributes of both Genders, but each sex will manifest most strongly those Gender attributes that are associated with their specific sex. The mind and the body are interrelated and co-dependent. Our thinking and our plumbing work together.

III
Gender in the Godhead

The universe is dependent on Gender for its existence, and since the universe is God's creation, within the Godhead there resides the seed for both the masculine Gender principle and the feminine Gender principle.

In the Kybalion, Hermes Trismegistus, one of the earliest influences on spiritual and philosophical thought, states that the "I" of our personalities is the creative Will of the masculine Gender, and the "AM" or "ME" is the nurturing and productive feminine Gender. When Moses asked how God was to be called, the response recorded in Exodus 3:14 is, "I AM the I AM". We can interpret this as, "I am the masculine and feminine Gender". There is no existence without Gender, therefore to say, "I am the masculine and feminine Gender," is to say, "I am all that there is."

Another biblical interpretation of Exodus 3:14 is that Gods' answer to Moses was "I AM BECOMING." This is also correct. The "I" is the unchangeable Will of God, which is a masculine principle. The universe is the plastic, pliable, changing, feminine principle. However, God is not changing, God is the unchangeable "I." What God has created is changing, that is what is "becoming"—that is the feminine principle of Gender.

The biblical allegory of woman being created from the rib of man is a colloquial explanation of the mystical truth that before a universe existed, there was no need for Gender; there was only the WILL of God, which is the masculine principle. When the universe was created, so was the need for Gender, and thus the feminine principle of existence came into being.

The mystical concept of the universe is that it is the mental projection of God. "ALL IS MIND" is a mystical axiom and a manifestation of the masculine Gender. However, the mind is cold, and life does not exist in the cold, it exists in warmth. That warmth is provided by the nurturing love of the feminine Gender. There is no electricity, magnetism, gravity, heat, no anything without Gender.

Jesus gave many examples of the masculine and feminine Gender principles. In the story of the woman taken in adultery he said, "Let he who has not sinned cast the first stone." This was the forgiving feminine Gender aspect of God. He also said at the same time and to the same woman," Go and sin no more". This was the demanding, standard setting, masculine Gender aspect of God. The story of the master, who forgave the debts of his servant, contains both the forgiving and retributive nature of God. In Oriental philosophy reference is made to the Yin and Yang of the universe; the Yang being the active, positive, masculine force, and the Yin being the passive, negative feminine force.

Is it not foolish to argue over the Gender of God, when it is obvious that both Genders emanate from God? The terms Mother Earth and the Father in Heaven, are used because the earth represents the unearned love of mother who feeds us all regardless of whether we are good or bad; and the earned love of father who tells us that if we abuse mother we will be punished. These terms are not to mean that the earth is mother and God is father, but rather that they represent the masculine and feminine aspects of God. God is as each person perceives God to be. Whether we call upon God as the Holy Father or Divine Mother, we are speaking to the same deity.

In the first half of the 20th century it was the masculine, Gender-based retributive and punitive perception of God that predominated in our worship, with the resultant guilt induced feelings, and suffocative effect on society. In the last half of the 20th century it has

24

been the feminine Gender-based forgiving perception of God that has predominated in our worship, with the resultant anything goes, do your own thing, chaotic effect on society.

When there is an imbalance of Gender, anywhere, in anything, in any organization, in any grouping of any life form, it will have a detrimental effect. Equanimity can only occur when there is a balance in the manifestation of masculine and feminine Gender.

IV
The Trinity of Accomplishment

Most major religions refer to the principle of the trinity. One manifestation of this principle is our accomplishments.

In order for anything to be accomplished there are three requirements. The Will to do, which is a manifestation of the masculine Gender; the creating and producing, which is the feminine Gender; and the medium through which accomplishment can manifest, which is called substance or matter.

The nature of all principles is that they are absolute and complete. There are no shadings or degrees in a principle. 2 and 2 is ALWAYS 4, it is never almost 4 or roughly 4. The acceleration of a falling body due to gravity is 32ft./second/second. Not usually, or most of the time, but always. A moving body keeps moving unless there is something to stop it—ALWAYS. A stationary body stays stationary unless there is something to move it—ALWAYS.

In the Universal Principle of Gender there is no such condition of mostly feminine or mostly masculine. The principle at work is purely masculine or purely feminine—all of the time.

Some illustrations of the principle of Gender at work and the resultant manifestation follow:

Masculine Assertive	Feminine Receptive	Manifestation
anode	cathode	electricity
sun	moon	light at night
north pole	south pole	magnetism
sperm	ova	child
farmer	earth	fruits and vegetables
bull	cow	milk
force	stillness	movement
force	movement	stillness
mind	law	order
goals	work	accomplishment
GOD'S WILL	human acceptance	spiritual attainment

In all of the illustrations the acceptance, receptivity, and compliance of the feminine Gender are total and without equivocation. The moon has no choice in reflecting the light of the sun. The ova has no choice as to which sperm will be impregnated in it. The earth has no choice as to the plants it will grow. Human beings have no choice as to God's Will.

The power of the masculine Gender is also total and unequivocal. The seeds were planted in the earth, the Sun shown on the moon, force was applied to the moving and stationery objects. There was no degree of application—just application.

The Gender principle is also at work within each person, and each person has access to all the attributes of both Genders. However, the nature of our bodies determines which attributes enable it to best function in harmony.

The body containing the receptive ova, the nurturing breasts, and the smaller more delicate stature draws unto it the feminine Gender attributes. The body that is broad at the shoulders and more muscular, and that generates what will impregnate the ova, will draw unto it the masculine Gender attributes. Even though each body has access to all the Gender attributes, those that assist and promote the harmony of the particular body will prevail.

To say that the "only" difference between a man and a woman are the organs of sex is akin to saying that the "only" difference between a giraffe and a rabbit is the size of the neck. The difference in the neck size affects the thinking, psyche and activities of these animals. It affects where they eat, how they eat, how they defend themselves, and the color of their skin. Their entire lives are different because of the difference in the size of their necks.

The difference in neck size is not nearly as different as the difference in Gender attributes. As Emmanuel Cellar, former congressman from Brooklyn said many years ago, "there is less difference between a chestnut horse and a horse chestnut, than between a man and a woman." Congressman Cellar was stating in colloquial terms the Universal Principle of Gender.

We have been taught that the amoeba, that one celled form of life, reproduces itself, a fact that seemingly negates the principle of Gender. This past year a notation in a magazine stated that scientists have "discovered" what appears to be Gender in the amoeba. Of course there is Gender in the production of the amoeba. Nothing is produced in our universe without the influence of Gender. It cannot be otherwise.

The masculine Gender wills and the feminine Gender produces. Nothing begins in until the masculine Gender Wills it, and nothing is accomplished until the feminine Gender produces it. Working in harmony together through the medium of substance, they create and produce all that is. It can be called the trinity of accomplishment.

V
Gender Relationships in the Animal World

The societal structure of the animal kingdom is based on Gender. The characteristics attributable to Gender define the function of the individual members of the grouping. These characteristics are the same for animals as for humans, for the attributes of Gender are universal, whether they apply to animals, humans, societies or organizations.

A species of the animal kingdom in which the Gender roles are clearly defined, and in which Gender differences are pronounced, is the lion. The role of the male lion is to determine the territory where the pride will live, taking into consideration the access to food and water, and its relative position to other prides. Once the territory has been determined, and been made known to lions of the pride and outside of the pride, the lioness then does the hunting and child rearing. Not only does she do the hunting, but once the kill is made, she and the cubs wait until the lion comes and picks out the choice parts for himself, before they eat.

The male lion assumes other aspects of government such as the acceptance of a new lioness and her cubs, or her unborn into the pride. If the males do not recognize her scent, her unborn cubs will be killed, for only the offspring of the males of the pride are permitted to survive. If the females recognize her scent, they will assist in the feeding of her cubs. The functioning of a pride of lions is based upon a tribal society in which Gender determines the role of its members.

We see in the male lion the attributes associated with masculine Gender such as; creativity—determining the location for the pride to live, pioneering—moving the pride to the new location, courage—ndicating to lions outside the pride the extent of the territory to be occupied by the pride, governance—determining the eligibility of members of the pride. In the lioness we see the attributes associated with the manifestation of the feminine Gender; nurturing—catering to the cubs and the lion, industriousness—doing the hunting, cooperation—assisting other lionesses with the feeding of their offspring, adaptability—catering to the new males that take over the leadership of the pride because they are stronger than the previous males.

There are those who do not appreciate the comparison of human behavior to that of animal behavior, the feeling being that we are far advanced from the animals. We aren't. The following paragraph describes a human situation in which the expected behavior was very similar to that of lions.

A strong, modern, liberated woman in her early thirties and employed in the film industry, and I met for cocktails to discuss a film script for which I was seeking the financing necessary to have it produced into a movie. During this meeting she suggested that we become partners, which was surprising to me, for we only knew each other casually before this meeting. She indicated to me that the film industry was a very competitive business that required almost ruthless negotiations. She felt that I had good business acumen, and that I was capable of dealing with the toughest negotiators. She had experience in all the different facets of film production, and felt that if I were to negotiate profitable deals with the film distributors, she would handle the production end. She said, "You cut the deal, and I'll do all the work." As I sat across the table and looked at her, I realized that she asked me to be the lion, and offered to be the lioness. This event was not unusual, it was natural and similar events occur every day between men and women. It is because of its naturalness that we tend not to notice it, but our Gender characteristics are an innate part of our natures.

A more elaborate form of societal structure than that of lions exists among baboons, which have a highly organized patriarchal societal structure called a troop. The members of the troop are subservient to a male leader who has a harem, and whose dietetic and sexual demands are catered to. This is a societal structure similar to most of the non-European world prior to the age of industrialization. One of the more interesting characteristics of the troop is that young adolescent males are encouraged to challenge the older larger males. After a few encounters of this sort, in which the young males end up being buffeted about by the older stronger males, they learn who the biggest and meanest baboons are, and then behave in a more subdued fashion, carrying out their respective roles in the support of the troop. Wouldn't it be equally beneficial, if retired football players, instead of being hired by food companies to screw lids on jam and pickle jars, spent time with our adolescent youth, and when the occasion required it, let them know who the strongest and meanest baboons were?

There is no form of organization, be it pride or troop, family, tribe, or nation, that can long endure without the governance of the masculine Gender. Leadership, rulership, and governance are masculine Gender functions, to have it otherwise is to court disaster. This disaster occurred in the economic sense in Eastern Europe and has occurred in the societal sense in America.

VI
Gender Differences
in Youth

I taught Sunday Church School to a group of teenage boys and girls who were in grades nine through eleven, came from upper middle class homes, and were getting an above average education.

One Sunday I gave them an assignment to observe the personal anxieties, hurts, aggravations, disappointments, and irritations of people, and to report on their observations the following Sunday. When we met again the following week, the girls reported a multitude of events: a passenger arguing with the bus driver, a teacher aggravated by a student, parents having an argument, a girlfriend upset because she thought her boyfriend was dating someone else, a neighbor worried about the possible result of medical tests, a neighbor whose employer might relocate worried about his job, on and on their reporting went, with what appeared to be a limitless number of observations. The boys had nothing to report. Nothing. I pressured them and asked if there wasn't anything that happened that was contrary to what they had hoped for or expected. Again nothing. Finally one of the boys raised his hand, and his wrinkled brow giving evidence of deep thought, said, "The Mets lost."

On another occasion I decided to inquire as to their feelings towards the opposite sex, and had girls only, on one Sunday and boys only, on another Sunday. In the session, which only the girls attended, I asked them why they went out with boys. The girls indicated that they eventually wanted to get married, and that going out with boys gave them an opportunity to determine if these boys would be good prospective mates. I asked what they use as measure of the boys qualifications for being a husband, and they indicated that comparing them to their fathers was a starting point. The girls knew why they were going out with boys, what kind of boys they preferred to go out with, how they expected them to behave, and what the final result would be. The following week I asked the boys why they went out with girls. Silence was the answer to my question. I asked again, and again I was answered with silence. I indicated that I knew that they went out with girls, because I had seen them with girls. I again asked why they went out with girls. Finally one of the boys said that he goes out with a girl when the other guys are going to a place where they bring girls. I then posed the question, "When you bring a girl to a place or party where the other guys bring girls, what traits do you like to see in that girl?" Silence. Finally after considerable probing, the same fellow who had expressed disappointment that the Mets had lost, raised his hand, and again his wrinkled brow giving evidence of deep thought (I presume he was the class intellectual) said that if he had to bring a girl on a date because the other guys were bringing one, then he wanted one "that wasn't jerky!" I asked the other boys if that was the kind of girl they wanted to go out with, "one that wasn't jerky", and they agreed unanimously. At that point I realized any further discussion of the opposite sex would be futile, as perhaps all the past discussion had been, and moved on to a new subject.

It was obvious that the girls were more mature than the boys; they knew that they were women, and were already attuned to the physical, social and material world that was a manifestation of the feminine Gender.

However, the boys were already well ahead of the girls in conceptual understanding, which is a manifestation of the masculine Gender. When the boys would discuss the big-bang theory of the creation of the universe, or the theory of black holes in space, the girls thought the boys were silly. Visual thinking, that is, thoughts that have size, form and color, were well manifested in the girls, whereas abstract thinking was already very evident with the boys. As we shall see in the following chapter, each sex had already developed the thinking necessary for them to accomplish their primary functions.

As far as the girls maturing earlier than the boys, in all species of life the superior intelligence always matures more slowly.

VII
The Physical Female

A woman's life is physical. The emotions she has are the result of physical thoughts and experiences. Her life revolves around her femaleness, and that femaleness is physical.

The primary difference between a woman and a man is that a woman is equipped mentally, physically and psychically for child bearing and nurturing. This ability and all that it entails is not a collateral function, but the primary attribute of her being, and all else is collateral. This is true whether or not she has children, for it is this nurturing ability that fuels the race.

Child-bearing to a man is a concept. Either instinctively or objectively, he realizes that the race must be propagated, or that he and/or his wife want a child. His creative Will, impregnated via his sperm into the nurturing female body and entering the ova, begins the process of propagation. Once the brief period required for the depositing of his sperm into the female has passed, the physical involvement of the male in the procreation of the race is ended.

It is the nurturing feminine aspect that will produce what the creative Will of the male has implanted. This nurturing is not a concept, but a highly physical process. From the moment of conceptualization, the female begins to change physically. Ovulation stops, she gains weight, her body goes through an almost infinite number of changes, she gives birth, her breasts swell, and she feeds her child. There is nothing abstract about this process. It is as physical an experience as exists. And this physical experience includes her surroundings, for she wants a safe, secure, sheltered, nest with the abundance of things necessary for her to nurture her child. It is said, "Women go where the money is." This is indirectly true. Women go to the material source that will provide the nest that they desire. A cave woman sought out the cave man who wielded the biggest club, who had the biggest and safest cave, and who could provide the most food. The female eagle mates with the male who has the largest wingspread, who can fly the fastest and farthest, who can build the most secure nest and protect it well. In the animal kingdom, if the females are not seeking out the strongest males, then it is the strongest males who are gathering up the females, but in either case, the offspring are being raised in the best material environment available. Amongst humans of this age, matters material are obtained with money. Therefore the modern woman, when seeking the male who can provide her with the material environment that she is accustomed to, or desires, mates with the most moneyed man she can get, who is compatible with her personality and other desires. In that sense "women go where the money is." There is nothing wrong with this concept provided that once the agreement to mate is reached, the woman maintains a relationship of loyalty and fidelity. Women seek to be with powerful men, this is as instinctive an action as mating itself, for it has its roots in the mating urge. It is assumed that the most powerful men will provide the most secure nest and abundant environment. The purpose of material things is to nurture the race, and it is the manifestation of the feminine Gender that is concerned with this nurturing.

A woman's life evolves around her being a female, and this too is a very material condition, From the age when menstruation begins, until the age when it ends, 20% of the days in a woman's life are attendant to that function. If she experiences premenstrual syndrome this figure may increase to 30%. To this can be added the time that she is concerned that her cycle is early, late or has stopped; the time spent on checking to determine if she is pregnant, why she isn't pregnant, and just being pregnant; the time spent on having her uterus and ovaries examined; the time spent on investigating various vaginal discharges; the time spent on mammary examinations; the time spent on various female surgical procedures, such as the removal of polyps, hysterectomies, and breast removals. On the occasion that there is no menstrual cycle, or concern with any aspect of it, that there are no health problems, that there is a regular day— if such a day exists—then she can be sure there will be any number of males around who would like to reach those parts that required her attention, and other parts as well. This creates another area of physical concern for a woman: the desirability of her body as determined by men. She therefore becomes concerned with the shape of her legs, hips, stomach, buttocks and bust, and spends considerable time doing what she can to make herself as desirable as possible. A woman's life revolves around her being a female, and the physical world that attends to her female necessities and responsibilities.

This physical nature of women has its effect on business and economics, and is in fact the basis for economics. The money spent on television advertising for products relating directly to the female requirements of women, exclusive of cosmetic needs, is in the hundreds of millions of dollars annually. Products for feminine hygiene consisting of tampons, pads, douches, deodorants are advertised on every TV channel, as are products related to the female cycle such as; medication for menstrual cramps, bloating, and premenstrual syndrome. Pregnancy tests, calcium supplements to combat osteoporosis, mammary gland inspection services, medication for the now seemingly ubiquitous yeast infections, are all products and services that exist to serve the female requirements of women. Is there even one product advertised on television that has to do with the male requirements of men? The servicing of the female requirements of women is a multi-billion dollar industry of physical products. The durable goods industry, which serves as one of the barometers of business activity, is actually an industry that serves the nurturing requirements of women. Are not products such as refrigerators, dishwashers, toasters, clothes washers and dryers, vacuum cleaners, blenders and stoves, all vehicles that enable a woman to nurture the race? Is not every product manufactured and advertised, for the nurturing of the race? Even the automobile, the primary purpose of which was to enable men to produce the products necessary for nurturing, has become a vehicle used by women to go about the process of obtaining the goods necessary for the nurturing of the race. The basis of economics, commerce, business, is the production of goods and services for the nurturing requirements of the race as performed by women, but are the result of the abstract thinking and creative Will of men.

The proliferation of female writers of books, articles and manuals on various self help subjects have taken the word "abundant" from the bible and enshrined it. We hear in lectures, and read in books and magazines, and see on public access television, pronouncements about the "Abundant" life the Lord has destined for us. We are encouraged to spend freely, charge a lot for our services, and in general to enjoy the "Abundant" life. Contrast this penchant for matters material with the life of men, whether they be warriors, Jesuits, adventurers, or scientists, who are admonished to "live a life without thought of material gain". Is it any wonder then that women think physically, that their thoughts are mental pictures that have form, size and color, whereas the thoughts of men are abstract and conceptual in nature?

As we shall see in the next chapter, it is this abstract, conceptual thinking coupled with the creative Will of men that creates and produces the products necessary for the nurturing of the race.

VIII
The Non-Physical Male

Men are taller, broader at the shoulders, narrower at the hips, more muscular, heavier and stronger, on the average, than are women. It could be said, that since men have the physical advantage over women, that it is the men who are very physical beings. As support for this viewpoint, it can be shown that males indulge in highly physical sports activities such as football, boxing, rugby, and wrestling. Males also excel in non-physical recreational activities such as chess, checkers, bridge, and other card games. A man's thinking is conceptual, the physical prowess that he has enable him to implement the product of his conceptual thinking.

During the evolution of the race, while the females were involved in child bearing and child rearing, the conceptual thinking of the males regarding how to provide for the preservation of the race, required considerable physical prowess in order for the results of that thinking to be implemented. Stamina, endurance and strength were required to climb mountains, cross rivers, develop new paths through forests and jungles, and defend against predator animals and unfriendly tribes. These activities, which required tremendous physical ability to accomplish, were the implementation of the creative Will. This creativity resulted in the abstract non-physical thinking that determined new paths to take, new sources of food, different methods of protection, inventions and their creative development, all of which benefited the race.

The physical thinking of women, the thinking in terms of form, size and color, are antithetical to creativity. A concept has no form size and color. Bell did not know what the telephone would look like, nor did Edison know what the phonograph would look like, indeed, the form, size and color of these inventions were changed shortly after they were invented. The prerequisites of inventiveness are not education and credentials, they are the exercise of the creative Will of the masculine Gender.

It is the continually diminishing influence of the masculine Gender that is causing the relative decrease in inventiveness in the last half of this century. During this same period the number of women graduates in engineering and the sciences has increased exponentially, yet their presence at the patent office is almost non-existent. Physical thinking does not create; it nurtures. Abstract thinking creates. Abstract thinking conceives. The abstract thinking and conceptualization of the masculine Gender, coupled with its creative will, produces the inventiveness that provides the products and services for the nurturing of the race.

IX
False Prophets

The religious texts were all written by men, therefore the teachings are sexist, is how the Feminist (those women who burn their bras, drop their pants and make sluthood fashionable) logic goes, or, as is more correct, how the lack of their logic goes. There are male followers and proponents of this lack of logic, who in many cases, are also opportunists who have capitalized on the influence of this thinking upon society.

These men purport to be the new, enlightened and sensitive men who are capable of reinterpreting the scriptures, be it the Torah, Bible, Tao, or whatever other scriptures are appropriate to their interests. They lecture, write articles, even books, about the tolerant nature of God, not the redemptive or forgiving nature, for these two qualities imply wrongdoing or sinful actions, whereas the tolerant nature of God implies that everything is all right. Their road show plays to a large audience of women who appear to be quite willing to fill the coffers of these false prophets.

There was a time when people would go to their clergyman to discuss actions that they had taken that they knew were wrong, and asked for advice, guidance and prayers of forgiveness. The new gurus have decided that this is no longer necessary because there is no sin. In Billy Graham's recent New York crusade in Central Park he lamented that the line dividing sinful living and good living had become a blur. He could just as well have said that it had been eradicated.

The proponents of this new philosophy have a growing following amongst women, for it absolves them of all responsibilities and obligations to authority and any feelings of guilt. Loyalty to the family, tribe and race is not included in their teachings. They have brought the philosophy of narcissism into religion, or have subverted religious teachings in order to justify narcissism. These false prophets take on the air of sensitive, understanding, loving men, who have not only a sympathy for women, but even an empathy for them. They may take on the air of an ascetic, even dress as one and eat as one. However, their asceticism does not extend to sex, which they will engage in with their devotees, even married ones, but not to worry, there is no evil in the eyes of the Lord as he watches us go about doing our own thing.

Men know these false prophets as wimps and weak-kneed milksops who suck on the production of society for their survival. They in no way have the characteristics to bring about positive change, for that is a manifestation of masculine Gender, something that is lacking in their make up. Religion was established through the efforts of strong, virile men who had the courage and pioneering spirit to espouse the spiritual teachings that were entrusted to them. These men went by the names: Abraham, Moses, John the Baptist, Peter, Paul, Mohammed, Martin Luther, John Welesly, and other names. They worked hard, gave an almost superhuman effort to their activities, faced danger continuously, and were frequently slain for their beliefs . Humankind benefited from their productive efforts. Wimps don't produce; they suck.

Concerning the consequences of the way we live, this is what a few famous men had to say:

"Whatsoever a man soweth, that shall he also reap"
—Jesus 30 A.D.

"Whatsoever a man soweth, that shall he also reap"
—Bidpai 300 B.C.

"Whatsoever a man soweth, that shall he also reap"
—Buddha 600 B.C.

"Whatsoever a man soweth, that shall he also reap"—Amenhotep
IV 1350 B.C.

They all said it. The mystical law of cause and effect, which in today's jargon means "what goes around, comes around". This law of cause and effect provides the punishment referred to in the mystical texts. We are punished as a result of our sins, not because of them. There is no escape from this law, no beating the system, except for true repentance.

To help us avoid having to learn everything the "hard way", guides for living were prepared by the enlightened masters in various parts of the world. These guides for living are called Holy Scriptures and indicate the "punishment" in store for us if we do not live our lives according to the guidance offered. Do we not use this very same approach in the raising of our children?

When at a pool club I observed a mother with a container of hot coffee and her young daughter at the wading pool. The mother had placed the container at the edge of the pool, and when she saw her daughter reach for it she said, "Don't drink it, it's hot." Still the child went after it, and her mother said, "Don't drink it, it's hot." The little girl picked it up, took a sip, and started to cry. The mother said, "I told you it was hot." Scriptures tell us what is best for us and what isn't; if like the little girl, we choose to not heed the advice that was given us, we pay the consequences.

In the mystical concept of existence, there is no such thing as good or bad, rather more evolved and less evolved, higher and lower, advanced, less advanced and more advanced. We are all evolving in our own way and at our own pace. Ultimately we shall all be saved and forgiven. However, until such time as we get there, we need the guidance and the warning of the scriptures. Also, until we get there, we need to survive here, and we need this guidance to coexist with our fellow man.

The event that motivated me to write this chapter was an interview of Stephen Mitchell, author of "The Gospel According to Jesus" and neo-interpreter of the Tao and Bible, which appeared in the November 1991 issue of Yoga Journal. One would think that a more appropriate title would have been "The Gospel According to Stephen Mitchell", but I guess that was too humble an approach for this new-age guru.

A few of the assertions by Mitchell during this interview were: Jesus is not divine; he was illegitimate; made mistakes; had self doubt; Paul was probably a Jew, but had his emotional problems; the mystical admonition to not give pearls to the swine or bread to the dogs, was intended for the gentiles, the Tao was sexist. That is saying a lot, considering that there wasn't any logic to support these assertions, but then logic doesn't exist in the non-masculine world. Men wrote all the books; therefore, they are sexist. How does one argue against that? Just as my wife used to say that people listened to me more than they did to her because I had the penis. Maybe, but I wasn't going to make any changes to alter that situation and accommodate her. The scriptures should not be altered either to accommodate the narcissistic philosophy of this day. Men wrote the scriptures because that's what men do. They also know how to deal with wolves in sheep's clothing and wimps who prey upon women.

X
The Gender of Economics

Economics has to do with the production, consumption and exchange of goods and services. The basic economic systems are capitalism and socialism; they are both western theories.

Capitalism calls upon the forces of the free market to determine the production, price and distribution of goods and services. It is predicated upon giving each person the opportunity to invest their time and money as they choose, and to reap the consequences of this action. In its purest sense it is fair and just. Capitalism is the Masculine Gender of economics.

Socialism calls upon government to decide upon the production, price and distribution of goods and services. It is predicated upon the economic sharing with all people according to their need. In its purest sense it is caring and nurturing. Socialism is the feminine Gender of economics. No one entity or system can long survive with a major imbalance of Gender, and this includes capitalism and socialism. Capitalism is cold, unfeeling and uncaring. A person gets what he or she earns. If they don't earn, they don't get. It makes for motivation, but not compassion. It is predicated upon the survival of the fittest, but makes no allowance for the unfit. Without the influence of feminine Gender capitalism will degenerate into barbarity.

Since the basis of Capitalism is freedom of action, the influence of the feminine Gender is also on a free basis, and it manifests itself as charity. Capitalism cannot survive without charity. Volunteers provide almost all of the caring and nurturing requirements of capitalist society. From the smallest town to the largest city, volunteerism is in action on a continuing basis. There is not a human being in Capitalist society that is not directly touched by the free giving of goods and services by individuals and groups for the benefit of others.

Socialism is non-motivating, uncreative and inefficient. It is predicated upon the survival of all, but makes no allowance for the unique wants, desires and contributions of the individual. Without the influence of a strong masculine Gender, Socialism will result in chaos. Since the basis of socialism is government control, and government is masculine in Gender, the viability of Socialism depends upon the strength of government, which is the military. Those nations that have Socialism without a strong military are nations in a state of chaos with a limited future. An exception to the need for a strong military role would be where the male segment of the populace was already conditioned to be extremely docile.

The nature of government—any government, is masculine in Gender. Capitalism has no affinity for government but instead has an affinity for the lack of government, which is feminine in nature. This is the reason that there is a resistance towards government intervention by capitalists. Still, government is required in order for any societal grouping to long survive. To the consternation of the conservative capitalists, the tendency of this government in the domestic sphere will tend to be feminine Gender influenced.

A more detailed discussion of government will be made in the chapter under that heading. Suffice it for now to realize that Gender influence exists in economics and government, and these institutions are always under the influence of both Genders.

XI
The Gender of Government

The Gender of government, any government, is masculine. The purpose of government is to govern. Even in our democracy, we speak of the consent of the governed. Being governed, or having a government, is a societal means of avoiding chaos. That function of governing is a masculine Gender function, a function for which the male is well equipped; mentally, physically and temperamentally; which is why the males of any species rule or govern.

One has only to observe the animal kingdom to understand what happens when the males are removed from any grouping. The females are left leaderless and consequently go about in all directions, aimlessly, until such time as a new male is able to take over the direction of the flock or herd. If the females are from a herbivorous species, they eventually become the dinner for the carnivorous species. The administration of a grouping is government, and that is a masculine Gender function. It does not exist without the masculine Gender.

Within that framework of government, both feminine and masculine influences exit, and as has been repeated, and will continually be repeated throughout this book, if a significant imbalance in this Gender influence occurs, there will be deleterious effects on that government.

There can never be complete agreement on the part of the sexes as to what constitutes a balance, for as one prospective female employee said to me "as I told my boyfriend, you men can never completely satisfy us, but that doesn't mean you shouldn't keep trying." (She didn't get the job.) The true test of relative Gender balance is the accomplishment, stability and evolvement of the race.

For some thirty years, at Chamber of Commerce lectures, political meetings, in magazines, on TV and in an assortment of Women's publications we heard of the wonders of the Soviet system and how there was no sex discrimination anywhere, how women were in all industries, at all management levels, involved in the entire economic process. Oh shame on us in America, that we were not doing the same.

Now the world is witnessing what has happened to that non-sexist society, there has been little accomplishment, instability is rampant, and about the only evolvement they can point to is that they understand that the economic system based on the negative aspects of feminine Gender has collapsed. But not to worry, the natural response of the female in times of difficulty is to turn to the male and say "do something." So now these proponents of all that failed are turning to the male chauvinist pigs of America, Japan and Germany (those nations that still have relatively more of a masculine Gender economy) and are saying "do something." This is what all organizations that have lost their masculine Gender leadership do, they turn to the most masculine Gender available and ask for help. That is what Chrysler Corp did, that is what the farmers do when they want subsidies. That is what self-help groups do (that's a real oxymoron isn't it.) That is what special interest groups do, especially the Feminists (those women who burn their bras, drop their pants, and make sluthood fashionable) who would be nothing without the legislation of government, that bastion of the manifestation of masculine Gender.

The same dissolution of the economy and government that is happening in Eastern Europe happens to all groupings or organizations that lose their masculine Gender influence. Families have deteriorated, crime has increased, special interest groups have proliferated, and society has become at odds with itself. What is happening to us is no different than what happens to a flock of chickens when the rooster is removed, there is chaos and disarray. The manifestation of the masculine Gender has decreased, and governing has become more difficult.

We will know that our government has reached a better balance of Gender when there is less crime, when we have fewer people in prison, when children born out of wedlock are a rarity, when SAT scores improve, when diverse groups are no longer divergent, and when the Feminist (those women who burn their bras, drop their pants, and make sluthood fashionable) movement is but a bad memory.

XII
Tyranny at Home

The period from the beginning of World War I to the Beginning of World War II was a time of extreme devotion to family, home, tradition, country, and faith, and the first half of this century was a time during which there was a strong manifestation of the masculine Gender. These two factors when combined caused an influence in society that resulted in order, loyalty, obedience, and devotion to the family, tribe, and race. It also ushered in an era of totalitarianism on all continents, and intolerance and prejudice in all religious, ethnic and racial groupings. Much has been said and written about this period in our history, but most of it in regard to the international scene. This period also saw a significant influence in the home, the results of which would have a negative effect on several subsequent generations.

An extreme of loyalty to a particular cause or group frequently results in prejudice towards those who do not believe in that particular cause, or who are not from that particular group. This condition existed not only on the international scene, but on the domestic scene as well. Good Catholic girls did not go out with non-catholic boys. Jewish boys would marry good Jewish girls. Chinese girls were forbidden to go out with non-Chinese boys. Good Greek girls would only marry Greek boys. Black girls didn't go out with white boys. And so it went, racial, religious and ethnic purity were high objectives in the loyalty to the family, tribe and race. It also made for a restricted social life for young people, especially girls, at least for the "good" girls.

The ultimate sanctity of any societal grouping is the purity and virtue of the females. The ultimate disrespect of a grouping is the defilement of their women, and the ultimate defilement is rape. In any war, the conquering army can be counted upon to rape the women of the conquered. This occurs not only because of the pent up sexual energy of the soldiers, but because of a desire to impress upon the defeated that they have been truly conquered, and what better way to make this impression than to have sex with their women.

The philosophy of having high standards for a societal grouping results in motivating that society to a high moral level, and it is only natural for the males to imbue their women with these standards, for these women will become the mothers of their children and the icon of the home. Not everyone could adhere to these standards, but as long as the standards were set at the average moral development of the race, most people could meet them. For those who could not meet these standards, be they men or women, there was always a man for every woman, and a woman for every man, regardless of their moral standing. This system allowed for a natural selection of mates while still having a moral standard, and worked very well, but when ethnic, racial and religious purity became a goal in a diverse society, problems arose.

In a society of diverse groupings, with a non-integrated social philosophy, ALL the women in a particular grouping suddenly became pure, virtuous and holy. This then meant that the males of any grouping, if they were to satisfy their carnal desires, would be doing so with females of another grouping—those who were not so pure. And while male promiscuity was more restricted than is generally imagined, it was more condoned than female promiscuity. However, it was only condoned if it were with women not of "their kind." Therefore, the promiscuous males of any grouping were having sex with females outside of their grouping. It sort of became a reenactment of the conquered and conquered. The women of the other group could be defiled, but not those of one's own group. Mathematics does not support the implementation of that philosophy and we can reasonably conclude that there had been a lot of acting and many guilty confessions on the wedding night. More importantly, the young married men were going to bed with those who were pure and saintly, and depending on the degree of matriarchal influence in their grouping, which as we shall see was much higher than was generally acknowledged, they were also going to bed with their mothers. This did not make for a natural connubial relationship, nor did it enable these males to exhibit the healthy, strong, virile manifestation of the masculine Gender necessary for the continued progress and evolvement of the race.

The focal point of society's devotion to the family, tribe and race, was the home. If there was any institution that was revered in the early part of this century, it was the home. Mom, apple pie and the home were symbolic of our racial, ethnic and religious devotion. Even criminals revered the home, for the home was sacred ground. Why didn't we think of dad and apple pie, or mom and dad and apple pie, or mom and dad and ham and eggs? The obvious reason is that dad wasn't there very much. The forty hour work week had not yet occurred. Dad usually worked six days a week and was often gone from the house 12 to 14 hours a day. This left dad time to do little more than eat and sleep at home. And while society at that time was essentially masculine Gender-oriented, and the men were Kings, their Kingship was not in the castle. The castle was ruled by the Queen, and rule she did.

Since dad was away, it was mom who was responsible for the total raising of the children. Mom saw to it that the children went to bed on time, got up on time, dressed appropriately, did their homework, had proper manners, respected everybody, had the right moral standards, worshiped regularly, and were always obedient. Some mothers could handle this load with love and understanding. Some became tyrants. They became tyrants not because they were bad women, but because they were ordinary women put in an unnatural situation; the unnatural situation being the relative absence of the positive attributes of the masculine Gender. These Tyrant Mothers had a profoundly adverse effect on their children, which would affect their interpersonal relationships and their ability to project the positive manifestations of their respective Genders. There were enough of these Tyrant Mothers that the combined adverse effect upon their children would create a severe negative effect on society, as these children became adults. It would affect interpersonal relationships, the concept of loyalty, and the positive manifestations of both masculine and feminine Gender.

The Tyrant Mother had an honorable goal—to raise "good" children. To accomplish this objective she worked tirelessly and maintained constant vigilance on the activities of her offspring. She was revered and respected by her husband, the schools, the clergy, the law, the medical profession, and any and all institutions that she came in contact with, for she was a woman who was devoting her life to raising "good" children.

Good" children performed well in school, and even if they weren't particularly bright, they still listened to the teacher and got an "A" in conduct. "Good" children dressed properly, were neat and clean, orderly, always finished their dinner, did their homework, were properly social, courteous, considerate of "others", selfless, respected all authority, especially the highest authority—Mother.

Mother operated from a powerful base—the kitchen. It was in the kitchen that Mom ruled with absolute authority. The kitchen furniture, decorations, china, and utensils were all purchased by Mom, as was the food. Mom stored things where she wanted, arranged the furniture the way she wanted, arranged dinner time to be when she wanted, cooked what she wanted, in the manner that she wanted. Except for poorer families in small apartments who might have used the kitchen as the family room and living room, even father was not permitted in the kitchen other than at meal times. From this base of absolute power, Mom's authority extended throughout the home. Her authority extended beyond the material aspect of the home, and engulfed the lives of all who lived in it. There was no room or activity that was not under the omnipresent eye of Mom. Mom checked on the homework, that the baths were taken, that the radio wasn't played too loudly, that bedtime was adhered to.

Mom supervised the social life of the children in minute detail. She decided who the good boys and girls were, and who could be played with and who couldn't. She determined if the children were acting socially proper, and if they were popular with their peer group.

Father's home life and social life was also under the direction and control of the Tyrant Mother. He lived in the home that his wife made for him, and had a social life that his wife created for him. It should come as no surprise that this era of the Tyrant Mother 1914 - 1945, was also the era of world wide gains in Women's Suffrage. The Women's Suffrage Movement succeeded by default during a time that men were little more than beasts of burden, and visitors in their own home. Women did not get equality with men; they filled in the vacuum left by men.

All of the aforementioned activities and objectives of the Tyrant Mother were activities and objectives that have been considered to be laudatory since the beginning of time. The reason that Mother became the Tyrant during this era is because of the imbalance of Gender that had manifested in the home. The extreme negative manifestation of masculine Gender is brutality, and the extreme negative manifestation of feminine Gender is extremism and cruelty. The Tyrant Mother, not answering to anyone, was extreme and cruel.

It was one thing to raise orderly children with high moral and ethical values, it was quite another thing to see orderliness progress to obedience, then compliance, then subservience. If there was any one characteristic that typified the child of the Tyrant Mother it was subservience. Subservience to the: teacher, priest, rabbi, minister, neighbor, company, employer, public servant, doctor, any adult, and especially mother.

All that her child did and accomplished was a result of the efforts and devotion of the Tyrant Mother. If her child was in the second grade and got straight A's on her report card, it was because mother saw to it that she studied. If she excelled in dance, it was because her mother took her to dancing school and made her practice at home. If he was courteous it was because of the training mother gave him. Whatever the accomplishment, it was because of mother, whatever the failure, it was because mother was not obeyed.

However, it was rare that the Tyrant Mother was not obeyed, for she had in her arsenal what seemed like an infinite supply of punishments. There were the basics, such as: severe scolding, grounding, spankings, and doing extra chores. Even the basic spanking given by the Tyrant Mother could be a very memorable event, depending on the weapon she chose to use. There was the old fashioned switch, the hair brush, cooking spoon, broom, shoe, or whatever was handy at the time. One 50 year old woman told me that she would remember a beating she received with a hair brush all her life, and while she couldn't remember what the beating was for, she did remember that she realized that she must never get mother angry. For the more sadistic Tyrant Mothers, there was making the children kneel on rice, locking them in closets, locking them out of the house, and sending them to bed without dinner. There was always public ridicule and condemnation, which was especially effective with female offspring. To pine in front of the neighbors, relations, or even total strangers, about the ungrateful, disobedient daughter that she had, this was the "what a martyr I am" approach. Or there was the yelling and screaming in public about the shortcomings of the girls, this was the "I will completely humiliate you" approach.

Occasionally there would be some adolescent daughter who would rebel, who would give evidence of having a "self", of being a person, who wanted to express her desires and feelings. For these hard core cases the Tyrant Mother would enlist the aid of the clergy, who themselves were in a control position in society and whose major supporters were the Tyrant Mothers, and whom they in turn would support in her efforts to cope with an unruly child. Also, there was the support of the Fourth Commandment, which read "thou shalt honor thy father and thy mother—Mother—MOTHER, all the days of thy life." So it was off to the Rabbi, Priest or Minister with the unruly daughter, and together mother and clergy would do the Mexican Hat Dance around her psyche until any semblance of self and womanhood were stamped out, and she returned home the subservient creature that she was raised to be.

Nor was there to be any help from father, who while a King outside of the castle, was a compliant serf when inside the castle. His advice when his children would complain about the overbearing mother would be, "You know you should listen to your mother, she means well" or, for the more timid and realistic, "You know you shouldn't get your mother angry". It is no surprise that these children would grow up with a resentment towards authority, and for many women a deep subconscious resentment towards male authority figures, not for what their fathers did, but for what they didn't do, for when they were in trouble and needed help, their fathers did not help them, but instead supported the tyranny that they were living under.

For boys there was the public slapping around, which usually was employed by mothers who did not have a man at home, or those who had husbands who were completely removed from the disciplining of their children. These mothers would beat their sons on the subway, bus, and street corner; or would come to the office in the morning and tell everybody how they chased their son around the house, beating him from room-to-room. Those mothers who did have a man at home who would administer punishment had the equivalent of a big obedient gorilla whom they could unleash on the children. An Italian-American friend of mine who was one of nine children told me that when his father came home from work, his mother would have all the children sitting in a circle around the living room, and then she would point to a "bad" one whom the father would then slam, then to another "bad" one who in turn would get slammed, then to a "so-so" one who would get a stiff kick in the rear to remind him or her what would happen if they progressed to "bad". So while many fathers might have administered discipline, they were in reality only the "hit men" or "enforcers" of the punishment meted out by the Tyrant Mother. It was only occasionally that a father might ask the question "if he asks me 'dad why are you beating me up' what do I say?" If the Tyrant Mother said a child was "bad", he was "bad", and there was nothing to question.

It could be said that the Tyrant Mother might have been overzealous, but she did motivate her children to achieve and succeed. This is a misconception, for her desire to have her children perform well was only while they were very young. A mother could take the credit for a second grader who got all A's, or danced well, or played an instrument well, or behaved well. But if those same children at the age of 17 got all A's, danced well, played an instrument well, or got a good job, most people would realize that it was a function of the ability of the child, and not much a result of the influence of the mother. Therefore, the Tyrant Mother began to underplay accomplishment and achievement as her children got older, and instead put the emphasis on social behavior, and on intangibles which were difficult to quantify. Perhaps her daughter got excellent grades in high school, so she was told that she didn't dress well, or didn't get invited to enough parties, or the right parties, or her hair never looked right. She was always compared to her peer group, and always came up lacking in the comparison. The common phrase of Tyrant Mothers was "you'll never amount to anything" or a sometime substitute when addressing their daughters "you'll never get married", which really meant the same as "you'll never amount to anything". This phrase was uttered by black and white mothers, Christian and Jewish mothers, Nordic and Latin mothers. Where it originated and what caused it to spread, I do not know, but I do know that the phrase "you'll never amount to anything" rang in the ears of all who were raised by Tyrant Mothers, and the effect on those generations was that they indeed contributed very little to society in the relative sense. This same attitude was manifested towards the boys as well, but the boys did get some respite, for boys had more opportunity to be out. They either had part-time jobs, were on school athletic teams, or were involved in sandlot sports of various types. Most mothers wanted boys out of the house, to be with "their own kind." The girls were not so fortunate.

As their daughters reached their teens, the Tyrant Mother's activities were focused on getting their daughters married. This met with the approval of the fathers and society in general, for in getting the daughter "married off", they in effect were soaking up the supply of single men and getting them into responsible productive situations, a necessity for the progress of society.

There were organizations at that time that provided facilities for teenagers that would enable the natural meeting and interrelating with the opposite sex. Various religious, ethnic and secular groups sponsored these organizations. Representative of the groups were: the CYO (Catholic Youth Organization) which would have dances in various churches on Friday nights; the GOYA (Greek Orthodox Youth of America) which would have formal regional dances; YMCA and YWHA; and the many Jewish Centers which would arrange various social events. These events were well chaperoned and provided a secure atmosphere for girls to begin to relate with boys, to "size them up", in preparation for the selection of a mate. Most boys were just beginning to "discover" girls and weren't as yet so sure why they related with them, but it was enjoyable, and they might even try it again. Most women who had the experience of attending these communal activities when they were girls, look back upon them with fond memories.

There were also unpleasant memories of these activities, which consisted of the reporting in to headquarters after the dance, of giving an account to the Tyrant Mother, of how popular she was, how many times she was asked to dance, and what prospects she unearthed for a steady boyfriend, which was the prelude to an engagement and then marriage. It was even worse if the Tyrant Mother attended the dance, for then the daughter would receive a first-hand, detailed accounting of how poorly she performed in relation to her peer group.

The belief that these mothers were preparing their daughters for marriage was another misconception. Their daughters were raised to be subservient to their mothers, and this subservience was expected to last the lifetime of the mothers. Getting their daughters married showed the competence of the Tyrant Mother in that she raised a marriageable daughter, and the marriage itself provided a vehicle that would rid her of the economic responsibility for her daughter.

Having attained the objective of getting her daughter married, and being free of any financial responsibility towards her, the Tyrant Mother could now devote the entire relationship with her daughter as the infallible critic of her flawed performances.

While there was tremendous effort expended by the Tyrant Mother to get her daughter married, there was hardly any effort expended on preparing her for marriage, except perhaps in the most negative sense. Advice such as "don't love him too much", "don't tell him everything", "don't expect too much from sex" (how could she, she didn't even know what it was) was the norm. Regarding her preparation for the prospect of pregnancy she had been told an assortment of quasi-truths and outright fabrications, which would give her little if any insight into the reality of the situation. "If a man touches you below the waist you'll get pregnant" was one. Having received this sage advice from her mother, a woman told me that when she was fourteen and at an amusement park with her girlfriends, a man fondled her below the waist. She told all her friends that she was pregnant, even after she eventually had a menstrual period, for the Tyrant Mother never told her that there was any connection between a menstrual period and pregnancy. "You'll know your pregnant when you don't have a period anymore", which while a step beyond the previous advice, left out some pertinent information. "If you're in a room with a man and he unzips his fly, you'll get pregnant", was at least a possibility. These quotes by themselves could be very humorous, however, when we consider that they pertain to the most important physical and emotional event of a woman's life, and that she didn't even know what caused it, is tragic. Under the tutelage of the Tyrant Mother it was not at all unusual for young college women to not know what caused pregnancy. No, the Tyrant Mother did not prepare her daughter for marriage, or any other situation involving interpersonal relations.

The grip of the Tyrant Mother over her sons was equally strong, and she would do her best to keep them from getting married, for the Oedipus Complex was very much alive, and she would manipulate and connive to keep some woman from getting her son. A Catholic

Tyrant Mother who would have gone into hysterics if her daughter had joined a convent, would have gone into ecstasy if her son had become a priest, for then she knew no other woman could have him. Usually there were only two women that the Tyrant Mother would not object to, the one her son had just broken off with, and the one he had not yet started to date. If she could not keep her son from getting married, she was sure to maintain her influence over him after he did.

So ingrained was the loyalty to the family, tribe and race, that the issue of the dominant mother was rarely discussed outside of one's tribal grouping, or more often than not, not even outside of one's family structure. On the occasions when it was discussed publicly, it was done halfheartedly or jovially, for good boys and girls did not talk negatively about their parents, especially when they became adults. This reticence to discuss the problems caused by one's suppressed childhood was also due to being objectively unaware of the issue. When Philip Roth's book *"Portnoy's Complaint"*, which contained specific abuses of the dominant mother, was published, it apparently surprised society that this condition existed, even though it was only Jewish people that were affected, or so society and for that matter the Jewish people thought. Jewish mothers were interviewed on television, for magazines and radio, as were experts on the Jewish culture. However, all these media people with their skilled interviewing ability never unearthed the fact that this same condition existed in other cultures. If Philip Roth had been black, black mothers would have been interviewed, if he had been Italian, Italian mothers would have been interviewed. The culture of the Tyrant Mother infiltrated households of all religious, ethnic and racial groupings; the tragedy being that the nation did not know it, but its effects would be manifest in every facet of our lives until the end of the century, and perhaps beyond.

XIII
Children of the
Tyrant Mother

The children of the Tyrant Mother had been raised to be concerned only with the feelings of their mothers, or others, never their own, and they had to strive to attain the goals established by mother, not their own. Also, the phrase that they heard so often in their youth "you'll never amount to anything", had taken a place deep into their subconscious. As a result these children had grown up without the ability to properly relate to others, and without specific goals.

There was also a difficulty in relating to women, on the part of both sexes. Many women raised by Tyrant Mothers, especially those without sisters, looked upon other women as competition and tended to be resentful of any of their accomplishments, for as little girls they were always compared to their peer group in an extremely competitive manner. Men raised by Tyrant Mothers did not know how to express differences of opinion to women without being intimidated, for expressing a difference of opinion to mother was rarely done, and then something undertaken with great risk. These children were ill prepared for the responsibilities of marriage, but the pressure on this group to marry early had been intense, and so they married, not infrequently to get out of the house of the Tyrant Mother.

People who are in an environment that they do not like, tend to leave it, move to a new location, and recreate that same environment, and then become angry with it. The children of the Tyrant Mother were no exceptions. The environment that they reproduced was that of their childhood, and in essence, they married their mothers, both men and women alike, creating a mutually masochistic relationship.

Self-preservation is a natural urge; especially preservation of the true self, not just the material body, and the children of the Tyrant Mother developed defense mechanisms to protect themselves from the abuse they experienced in their youth. There are three basic defenses: to be so good as to never get scolded, to be so belligerent so as to intimidate others, to control all expressions of feeling to prevent the possibility of being hurt.

People who used the first of these defenses always did what they thought was expected of them, and if they didn't know what was expected, they did nothing. I knew a woman who in middle age would say to her husband "tell me what to do". Mother had always told her what to do, and now she was expecting her new mother to do likewise. People who used the second of these defenses would talk to others arrogantly, or in a tough aggressive manner. I knew a man who could make "good morning" sound like a challenge. He was really a warmhearted fellow, but the gruff exterior was his means of protection. People who used the third of these defenses never showed emotion. They had it but they keep it a secret. They didn't get angry, happy, sad or frightened. They didn't experience love either. Everyone uses a combination of these defenses, sometimes one predominates, sometimes another.

Recreating the environment that they did not like, and bringing into that environment the defense mechanisms that they had developed, did not make for happy or successful marriages. These marriages produced an environment that was no better for their children than was the environment created by the Tyrant Mother. This environment contained parents who had difficulty relating to each other, mothers who were not happy with their womanhood, fathers who could not cope with family responsibilities, parents who committed adultery, or became involved in substance abuse, and who usually got divorced.

The environment created by the Tyrant Mother became the spawning grounds for the Feminists (those women who burn their bras, drop their pants and make sluthood fashionable) who resented all forms of authority, especially male authority figures whom they blamed for all their woes. It also spawned homosexuality on the part of both sexes, for these children were raised to be insecure with their sexuality, and the opposite sex became a threat to them.

My original manuscript stopped at this point in its description of the personal hurt that was a result of being raised by the Tyrant Mother, because most of us do not like to be reminded of the deep hurt within ourselves, and there is a tendency to reject the truth of this hurt and to resent those who are reminding us of it. However, the negative effect on the womanhood and the manhood of those who were raised in this environment is so intense, and has so effected our societal order, that I have decided that regardless of the personal animosity that might develop towards me, to proceed with a more detailed description of the effects of the Tyrant Mother on her grown children. Also, being a man, I am naturally more aware and concerned with these effects on women, and while I will attempt to make an equal analysis on the part of the men, I will probably fall short of the mark.

All people want to be close to mother, for mother is the source of our entry into this world and our physical link to the Almighty. She is also the source of the nurturing love that we all require. However, as much as we desire to be close to the Tyrant Mother, we know that if we get too close, she might reach out and claw us. Therefore we get almost close, near but not intimate-no touching. One of the more visible signs of the daughters of the Tyrant Mother, is that they they don't touch. They have sex, but no affection. They can give their bodies but not their hearts, for to open one's heart is to be open to hurt. They adopt the credo of the hooker "don't kiss a man on his lips", for to kiss on man on his lips is to express affection, to kiss him elsewhere is sexual stimulation. For these women, sex is akin to a good bowel movement, when its over you flush it away. Whereas to give one's heart has a lingering effect, and for as long as the heart is open, there is the chance of being hurt. Better to close the heart and not be hurt. Then they wonder why they can't find love.

These women will go to great lengths to avoid intimate relationships, all the while claiming that they do want intimacy but cannot find the right man. One woman who had never married told me that her first serious relationship was with a married man, her second serious relationship was with a priest, her third serious relationship was with a man so unsuited for her that anyone seeing them together would recognize it. She volunteered that she had picked men in her life with whom she knew she could not have a long term relationship. I met a woman who had been divorced seven times, and she admitted to me that all the marriage failures were her fault. She expected men to cater to her feelings, but as she said, "Not only did I not cater to their feelings, I wasn't even aware that they had feelings to cater to". I met another woman who had never married but who had been engaged to 11 different men. These cases may be extreme, but they indicate the extent some women will go to in order to avoid intimate and lasting relationships. More frequently we will see women who have been divorced at least once, and who have had a series of lovers but no lasting relationships. To use the word "lover" here is really is a misnomer, for if there is anything these women cannot handle, it is love. These men are sex partners at best, and users at worst. The relationships are arrangements of temporary convenience, not loving relationships. Some women are so fearful of having a close relationship that they deliberately portray themselves as women of promiscuity in order to ward off the attention of a man whom they fear they might "fall for".

These women are jumping on and off the merry-go-round of male contacts. When they are off the merry-go-round they are lonely, so they jump on to find a man. If they find a man whom they can love, they get scared and jump off. If they find a man whom they do not love, they have a relationship, but a relationship without love becomes boredom, and they eventually jump off. As what they perceive as a critical age approaches, whether it be 40, 50 or 60, they panic and jump on and off the merry-go round with increasing frequency. It gets them nowhere because their choice of men ensures failure.

At a lecture on "*The Course in Miracles*," Marianne Williamson, in addressing the women said, "You ask why is it the insensitive men call me, the men who won't make commitments call me, the men who are looking for their own self gratification call me, why is it that these men call me"? And she gave them the answer, "Because they are the ones to whom you gave your number". Yes, these women were seeking out what they subconsciously wanted, a non-close relationship, a superficial relationship, a non-committal relationship. And they got it.

There was a time when women wanted a man to want them for their entire beings, not just for sex. They realized that sex was just a part of the greater intimacy of a love relationship. Today, the daughters of the Tyrant Mothers can give sex, but not their hearts. Some of them even speak of lovers and friends, as though the lover could not be a friend. Of course if the lover becomes a friend, then there is the danger of love and hurt. There is a real sadness in this, for they are willing to forgo love in order to insure not being hurt. There is also tragedy in this, in that these relationships are a form of masochism, for to have sex with a man who has no feelings for the woman, is to be used and abused by him. This is a replay of childhood, being punished by mother for seeking out your own personal joy.

Sex without love at best is sensation, and sensation never satisfies beyond the moment. Sex with love is joy; anything with love is joy, for love is not a sensation, but the nurturing power of the universe. All things work well when accompanied by love. Very little goes well without love. Love must be experienced to be known, and once experienced, all else in life becomes secondary.

It is the tragedy of our time that so many women, whose God-given nature is to nourish, are unable to do so as a result of the suppressive nature of their childhoods. This condition is compounded by the hedonistic philosophy that pervades all media and preaches sex without love. Consequently they are on a narcissistic road to self-aggrandizement that results in their being abused, disrespected, and lonely.

As you read this my sisters, some of you will become very angry because I have gotten too close to home and you cannot endure the hurt of looking at this condition. Some of you will cry because you recognize the condition but are not yet ready to do anything about it, and some of you will be motivated to do something. Once we recognize there is an issue to be resolved we do something. For those of you who have been motivated to do something, I am happy that I was a part of it. To all of you, as I write this, my eyes are filled with tears as I think of the hurts and disappointments you experience and the humiliation that you are subjected to. Remember my sisters you were not put on this earth to be a slave to the passions of man, but to be his reasonable companion. Learn the difference between giving and being abused, and give fully to the man of your choice. Do not get caught up in the narcissistic philosophy, but instead think of being able to fulfill your responsibilities so that the men will be more readily able to fulfill theirs and together you will work toward and share in, the nurturing and evolvement of the race. I send my love to all of you.

To my brothers who are the product of the Tyrant Mothers, you too have avoided closeness by not allowing women to get close to you or choosing women who will disrespect you or abuse you. Yes, there are women who abuse men, not only in the overt manner of scratching, kicking and beating, but in the covert manner of manipulating the man to be the abuser. The masochist always wins; the person who is whipped gets our sympathies; the person with the whip draws our ire. Also, the woman who continually ridicules her man is abusing him. And just as women give their phone numbers to the wrong man, men ask for the phone numbers of the wrong women. However, because men are out of the home more, and more oriented to accomplishment in the material and professional worlds, the effects of their Tyrant Mother childhoods are not readily apparent, but if we reflect on their business behavior, we will see expressed the devastating effects of their childhood environment.

One of the characteristics of the child of the Tyrant Mother is the inability to relate to others easily, especially in the area of expressing desires and differences. This makes for erratic leadership in any profession or activity. It is difficult for these men to lead, motivate, and inspire. It is difficult for these men to set goals as well, for mother always set the goals at home. The phrase "you'll never amount to anything" was burned deep into the subconscious of many men, and when the moment for action was at hand, they "could not pull the trigger". Even among the many intelligent, educated and ambitious men of the Tyrant Mother, success seems to be elusive. Unfocused, unassertive and filled with self-doubt, these men failed to live up to their potential, and the family and nation lost accordingly.

The environment created by the children of the Tyrant Mothers became the spawning grounds for the wimp generation. The wimp generation complained about everything: they were raised in a bad marriage so why risk getting married; the price of homes is out of reach, so why save for a home; they are ethnic minorities, so they need special treatment; they are racial minorities, so they need special treatment; they are chronological minorities, so they need special treatment; they are women, so they need special treatment. Everybody needs special treatment, and if they don't get it, if they are abused, they can always sue. This generation can also be known as the "I'll sue you" generation, for they have brought the number of civil suits to unprecedented levels, and with charges that are beyond all credulity. Litigation today also offers the greatest incentive to financial success, providing a huge return on investment. Is it any wonder then, that we are becoming less productive as a nation?

Is it any wonder that as a nation, our loyalty to the family, tribe and race has decreased? Is it any wonder that in sports the free agent came into being, that people change jobs more frequently, that disco dancing replaced ballroom dancing, that the aged live in special places, that the young are in day care centers, that married couples pursue independent careers, that everyone is out for themselves? Is it any wonder that we are living in a vacuous narcissistic society?

And who is to blame for these conditions? No one. Not even the Tyrant Mother. She maintained high standards, was a tireless worker, was faithful to her husband, devoted to her family, and embraced the moral standards of society. The condition that caused mother to become the Tyrant Mother was the relative absence of the manifestation of masculine Gender from the home, creating a Gender imbalance and the excesses that resulted from it.

The men are not to be blamed either, they went about doing what they always did, doing what they had to do to best serve the family, race and the tribe, which at that time was going off to work in the factories, mines, and oil fields of the second industrial revolution. As mentioned in other chapters in more detail, they created immense wealth and leveled up the material lot of the entire nation to unprecedented heights. No one at that time realized what effect their absence from the home would have on succeeding generations, and on the nation.

XIV
You've Not Come
a Long Way Baby

The phrase "You've come a long way baby" is a travesty of logic that has produced an enigma in the consciousness of this nation.

The phrase refers to the apparent progress that women have made in this century by no longer being under the influence of their husbands, at least as it regards the freedom to smoke cigarettes. They can now smoke as much as they want at will, and therefore have come a long way since the time when husbands restricted their smoking. Women now have an increasing incidence of lung cancer, and other smoking related illnesses, and their life spans are now shortening in relation to those of men. It would be appropriate if, after an examination for lung cancer the results are positive, the physician then advise the woman of the results by handing her a card from Virginia Slims which states "you've come a long way baby". When it's time for her funeral, a sticker should be placed on the coffin saying "farewell, you've come a long way baby", courtesy of Virginia Slims.

This advertising incongruity pertains not only to the smoking of cigarettes by women, but also to their freedom from all their suppressions, real or imagined. They now drink alcoholic beverages more than when they were under the watchful eye of their husbands, and having come a long way, now have an increasing incidence of cirrhosis of the liver.

Women are no longer under the sexual restraint of their husbands or fathers, and having come a long way, those with human papiloma virus and chalmydia now number in the millions. These are venereal diseases that can be quite painful to a woman and also inhibit pregnancy.

Women are no longer segregated from men in college dorms, and having come a long way now experience an incidence of rape on campus that, at some colleges has reached epidemic proportions.

Since there are no restraints on the vocation a woman may choose, and especially since we no longer have any activity known as sinful, having come a long way, more women are induced to participate in pornographic activity and prostitution, with the resultant physical, mental and psychic debilitation.

It is no longer considered necessary to be married to have children. Unwed motherhood is even encouraged by the government by its welfare policy. Having come a long way baby, 25% of the children of our nation are born out of wedlock and raised without a male role model. This eventually produces stress in the mother and the children, resulting in a multitude of personal and societal problems.

Having come a long way baby, mothers now pass on to the unborn fetus, substance addiction problems.

Having come a long way baby, more women live alone, have no masculine presence in their lives, are lonely and stressed out.

Having come a long way baby has produced a generation of women who are apprehensive about their safety, who are being harassed and raped, whose lungs, liver and wombs are rotting away, whose children's minds are stunted, and whose sons are being shot dead in the streets or sent off to jail.

Coming a long way baby has produced a social disaster of a magnitude that only the conquering enemy used to inflict. There is no amount of government regulation that will alter this situation. There is only one species of human life that protects and cares for women and children. That species is called MAN. Until society recognizes the primary male role and supports it, the race will continue on its downward spiral.

YOU HAVE NOT COME A LONG WAY BABY

XV
The Myth of
Traditional Male Jobs

We often hear that women are making significant inroads into traditional male jobs, and given equal opportunity in these jobs, they will be able to perform as well as men and rise to the same heights as men.

What is a traditional male job?

Is it farming? Milking cows? Churning butter?

Is it transportation? Riding horses? Driving wagons, cars, buses, trucks or planes?

Is it manufacturing? Making pottery, ice boxes, refrigerators, computers?

Is it medicine? Nursing? Being a physician? Performing surgery?

Is it education? Being a teacher? A professor? A principal?

Is it the culinary arts? Being a cook? A chef?

Is it fashion? Being a cutter? Pattern maker? Designer?

Is it business? Being an entrepreneur, shopkeeper or CEO of a large corporation?

How is a traditional male vocation defined?

It cannot be defined, because there is none.

What is traditional amongst males is the masculine gender trait to pioneer, risk and create.

Once the pioneering has been done, the risk taking completed, and the creativity accomplished, the continuing work is then opened to women.

Men learned to ride horses, and then they taught women to ride horses. Men invented the wagon, they first drove it, and once it became an accepted means of transportation, women then drove wagons too. Men invented the car, and once it was pioneered, women began to learn to drive. A similar evolvement occurred with the plane and the ship.

Man milked the first cow and then taught women to do it. He invented the churn and then she churned butter. He invented milk machines and the dairy, and now she operates a dairy.

In the manufacturing field, after mass production was developed, pioneered and all the risks taken, women were then introduced to the assembly line. Women are more proficient at this type of work than men are, because work per se, and routine especially, is not a masculine Gender manifestation. Women have always done most of the work, they do most of the work now, and they always will. Man no longer belongs in the factory. He has pioneered its use. It's time for him to move on to other things.

In the field of medicine, the nurturing caring aspect of the female gender was always recognized and appreciated, nevertheless the creative aspect was a male function, and the use of the results of this creativity was then turned over to women. Men first performed surgery, and then women were trained. So it was and is in every branch of medicine including obstetrics, gynecology and pediatrics.

In education we have had female teachers for centuries. They taught the knowledge that men had developed, from books that men had written, with language that men had created and organized.

Why is it that men excel in the culinary arts, in fashion, in the performing arts? Men even dominate dance and music, which are primarily expressions of the feminine Gender. Most choreographers, songwriters, composers are men. Men excel in these fields because creativity, the pioneering spirit, and risk taking are primarily masculine Gender attributes.

In the field of business, and especially in the activities of the true entrepreneur, we see the results and benefits of the risk taking, pioneering, creative urge. As has been said earlier, Capitalism is a masculine Gender concept, and in its purest sense allows for the maximum creative outlet. It is here that men risk all, spending their last penny, and all that they have been able to borrow as well, in the development of new products and industries, and in the process creating unimagined wealth for humankind. After the pioneering, risk taking, and creativity are completed, then women work in these organizations, while the men move on to new fields of development.

In all the diatribe about women being able to do men's work, the focus is that they can do what men can do too. They can drive too. They can perform surgery too. They can fly planes too. That too, means they are following not leading. They are not prone to create too, or pioneer too, or take risks too. Or at least not to the degree that men can. And those few women who can, are readily recognized by men and need no laws or credentials to confirm their ability.

The "donkey mentality" ascribed to men by the laws of this nation is a disgrace. When work is too heavy, or too big, or too cumbersome for a woman in one way or another, then a man can be called forth and paid more to do it. That is if a donkey isn't available.

How about propagating a creative mentality, a getting it done against all obstacles mentality, a pioneering mentality, a risk taking mentality?

The listing of biblical genealogies according to male parenthood is considered to be a result of chauvinistic male writers. Do livestock breeders breed according to the bible or economics? Heifers are mated with prize bulls and mares with prize stallions. The reverse cannot be made to happen. The creative will is a male Gender function that permeates all existence. Even the process of fertilization, that act of all the multitude of sperm forging ahead, competing, pushing, striving to be the one successful entrant into the female egg is representative of the manifestations of the masculine Gender.

There is no such thing as a traditional male job. There is only the traditional manifestation of the masculine Gender. In the economic realm, the male role will be to create new products, pioneer new methods of providing goods and services, and uncover new resources. He will be using the inherent tools of his masculine Gender to provide for the propagation and preservation of the species.

In the first half of this century when the pendulum of Gender was swinging in the masculine direction, the automobile, plane, telephone, phonograph, motion picture camera, radio, television, sonar, radar, computer, atomic power, jet propulsion, and space satellites were all invented. In the last half of this century when the pendulum of Gender was swinging in the feminine direction, we saw the application, development, and assimilation of these inventions on a worldwide basis.

Just as no individual can be continually creative, society and the world need a respite from creativity in order to have time for assimilation. The first half of this century provided a lot to be assimilated, perhaps it took the last half of this century to complete that task.

Society is now clamoring for another creative thrust in the economic realm. There are huge requirements for food, energy, and transportation. There must be new ways of attaining these products. They can only be attained by the free creative will of the masculine Gender.

As we will see in the following chapter, there is no such thing as like work, especially between the sexes, and our attempt to enforce the myth of like pay for like work, has produced a deleterious effect on our productive ability.

XVI
The Myth of
Like Pay for Like Work

The day that I started to write this chapter a market on 86th Street and Broadway had blueberries on sale for $1.99 a pint. I bought my blueberries earlier that day at a market on 77th Street and Broadway for 88 cents a pint. Two weeks earlier, the market on 86th Street sold apple juice in two quart bottles for $1.99 each, while the market on 77th Street was selling the same brand for $3.49 a bottle.

We are all accustomed to the fact that there is no such thing as like product for like price. Price is determined by the open market, by what the consumer is willing to pay at a given time. The price for air conditioners and swimming pools is less in the winter than in the summer. The price for tomatoes out of season is higher than the price in season.

Employee wages are also a variable in a free market economy. A secretary living two blocks from her office would be willing to work for less than one who has to travel an hour and a half to and from her job. A copywriter's place of employment that is only ten minutes from a college she is attending nights, will get her services for less than would a similar firm an hour from the college. A married couple with children who decide to work separate shifts in order to always have someone at home, might work for less than those who can choose the shift they want.

There are employers who have pleasant working conditions, and those who don't. There are those who have liberal benefits and those who don't. These factors all influence the price for which we are willing to sell our services.

To locate a factory near the suburbs usually means a plentiful supply of office help at low cost, but a shortage of unskilled factory help at high cost. To locate the factory in the inner city will result in low cost factory help, but high cost secretarial help.

There are also preferences of personality. Some people dislike commuting while others enjoy it. Some like to work days, others nights. Some like to work inside, others outside, some in groups, some alone. In a free economy there is a rich and varied source of employment available at differing pay scales. Like pay for like work is more unlikely than likely.

As companies grow, and there is more than one person in a given job category, an attempt at fairness dictates equal starting salaries, but this is a function of administration, not economics. The larger that companies become, the more they reward employees for administrative reasons rather than economic reasons. We will discuss the negative results of administration on the creative process later. For now let it suffice that like work for like pay is not a basic economic concept.

Since the thrust of this book is on the difference of Gender and its proper application, this chapter will also deal with these differences in the workplace.

As a prelude, I will relate an event that happened in the early years of my marriage. My wife went to a beauty salon that had four female hairdressers, Sue, the proprietress and three employees. When she arrived at the salon only Sue and one employee were there. My wife's appointment was with Sue, and as she was doing my wife's hair she explained that one hairdresser was at the obstetrician because she was pregnant, the other was at the gynecologist because she couldn't get pregnant, and that she herself had severe menstrual cramps and only came to work because she knew the other two would be out. When my wife came home she said that if that had been a barbershop with four male barbers, maybe one of them would have had a cold. That little event illustrates the differences of Gender in the workplace.

That incident was not an aberration, but the norm in business. I owned and operated a sewing and heat sealing business for 23 years, and had both male and female employees. Some of the female disorders which I can still remember are: one hysterectomy, one radical surgery, two polyp removals, two closing of the tubes to avoid pregnancy, one twisted womb, various pregnancies, and one case of swelling and bloating outside of the menstrual cycle. If any of my male employees ever went to see a urologist, I am unaware of it.

There were various domestic and emotional situations affecting the performance of the women such as husbands leaving the wives, or maybe worse, husbands returning, and boyfriends leaving and returning. There was the occasional rape and its traumatic effect. Mom might leave and the baby-sitting facilities would leave with her. Sister might arrive for n extended visit making increased demands upon her. The husband or boyfriend returning and deciding that they were going to move elsewhere. Women had most of the accidents, and I can confirm insurance company statistics that most of these accidents occurred between the start of PMS and the end of the menstrual cycle (I asked and they told me).

Concerning the actual performance of a given job function, the women usually performed better than did the men. They worked faster, neater, and more consistently. If the workplace wasn't too hot or cold, too light or dark, reasonably clean and quiet, and if they had another woman to talk to (my machines were ideal for the women, as two operators were required for each machine) they became contented productive workers. Think back to the earlier analogy of the lion and the lioness. Once the territory was defined and protected by the lion, the lioness took over the work.

The male workers on the other hand were not as contented and only rarely matched the production rates of women. I did have a couple of real macho men who would not let it be said that a woman could out produce them. This kept my shop productivity rate higher than any incentive system I could have devised.

While the individual piece rate of men tended to not be as high as that of women, nevertheless, the men developed every labor saving, productivity improving, and cost reducing innovation. These innovations were further examples of male creativity on the job. The men did not like being machine operators. They liked handling material, cutting, boxing, unloading and loading trucks, inspecting, and any other tasks that allowed for them to use some innovation and creativity, that allowed them to set their own pace, or allowed them some flexibility in attaining the pace that management expected. It was the men who wanted to make changes; to move the machines, the cutting tables, the inspection tables, the time clock, the lunch room, the building itself. The women didn't want anything moved or changed. Once they were accustomed to where everything was, they resisted all change.

This was true in the office as well as the shop. It took me six weeks to convince a highly competent bookkeeper to let me buy a postage machine that automatically sealed and franked the envelopes. She was quite content to lick the envelopes and use the hand crank type machine for the postage. Years later, when I bought a computer, there was almost a revolution in the office, as the women did not like that I brought "that thing" into their work environment.

In light of the foregoing examples, is there any validity to the statement that the sexes do like work? Obviously then, there can be no such thing as like pay for like work.

The purpose of this article is not to conclude whether the men or the women are better employees. That would be like trying to determine which is the better Gender of the universe. There is no such thing as a better Gender. There is however, recognition of Gender in all things, and the proper application of that Gender. We need in the workplace the creative, pioneering, risk taking attributes of the masculine Gender, and the industrious, harmonizing, cooperative attributes of the feminine Gender. The pay scales should reflect the need and availability of these traits.

Women will be accounting for a larger and larger share of the labor force. This can be done naturally and without "minority" hiring quotas. Men will be leaving the more routine jobs and gravitating towards those jobs that require a greater degree of manifestation of the masculine Gender.

The unnatural influence in the work force is the policy of credentialism, which, as we shall see in the following chapter, is choking off the opportunities for masculine creativity.

XVII
The Aristocracy
of Credentialism

Credentials are used to confer authenticity, legitimacy, and basic capability to individuals and institutions that are not normally participants in the free market economy.

Some people choose to practice medicine, law, professional engineering, accounting, teaching, and other professions. Some institutions requiring credentials are hospitals, schools, restaurants, barbershops, or any enterprise or facility that serves the public. The purpose of these credentials is to protect the public by verifying the course of study, and professional experience of the practitioner, and the minimum standards of the establishment wherein they perform their practice. Credentials are not normally used as a measure of ability beyond what was required to earn the credential.

Performance serves as the measure of ability in a free market; however, in the case of the professions, we either do not use their services often enough to evaluate performance, or once we try their services to see how they perform, we are unable to do anything about the performance. A patient has only one opportunity to evaluate how an appendectomy was performed on himself. An accused usually has only one opportunity to be defended in court.

The method whereby performance is determined in the professions is by reputation, and this reputation is made known to the client by referral. My dental requirements are taken care of by two highly competent dentists. When I needed root canal therapy they sent me to a highly competent endodontist, and when I required periodontal treatment, they sent me to a highly competent periodontist. Birds of a feather usually flock together, and people of similar competence associate together professionally.

It is performance that determines the desirability of services and/or, products. Outside of the professions, the free market determines what we think of performance. Within the professions, referrals are the measure of performance. A competent accountant will be able to recommend a competent lawyer, and a competent engineer will be able to recommend a competent contractor. Performance guides the free market economy.

The free market economy is also a manifestation of the masculine Gender, and performance is the gauge by which men measure one another. The respect, admiration and recognition that men have for each other are based on performance, a performance that results in accomplishment. Men are judged by their peers on a continual basis regarding performance and accomplishment.

These peer standards of performance permeate all aspects of a man's societal involvement, whether it be in war, sports, business or the home and family.

In warfare, it matters not what credentials a soldier has, what matters is how he performed in combat. If the performance was exemplary, he gets a medal. Napoleon was chided by one of his ministers for spending so much time pinning those little tin medals on his troops. Napoleon's response was that great battles are won and lost by these little tin medals. What German officer in World War II did not want the Iron Cross? He was motivated to become daring and heroic at the cost of his very life, just to earn the right to wear that little tin medal, because it represented to him recognition by his peer group.

In sports, players are paid for the tackles they make, the touchdowns they score, the home runs they hit. Their performance on the playing field is no different than it was on the battlefield. They are expected to perform, and when the performance is exemplary they are recognized. They are recognized not only with salary and bonuses, but with rings, trophies, belts and pins—the little tin medals of the sports world.

In business, depending on the position that a man has, he is recognized for the profits produced, the new products developed, the new plant completed on time, the cost reductions made, the sales goal achieved. He is rewarded not only with money and position, but with watches, pins, plaques and trophies—the little tin medals of the business world.

In the familial or tribal sense a man is judged by the house he can provide his wife with, the schools he can send his children to, the vacations the family takes, the medical care he provides, the jewels he can adorn his wife with—and which she wears in public—for they are the little tin medals of familial recognition.

This recognition of accomplishment extends to small boys. Before the advent of Little League activities (one of the early manifestations of the swing to feminine Gender influence) when boys played baseball, the peer group knew who the best performers were, the two best would be the captains, and they would alternately choose the players to be on their team. The sequence in which the teammates were picked was predicated upon their performance as recognized by the peer group in general, and the two captains in particular. Too bad if little fat boy could hardly run, then he became one of the last picks, and played in a least vulnerable position, usually between two stars who could take up the slack he created. Too bad for little skinny boy who could hardly pick up the bat, he was placed at the bottom of the batting order.

Love and consideration exist among males, but it must be earned. If little fat boy persevered, and one day beat out a bunt to first base, all the boys stood up and cheered. If little skinny boy hit a triple to the opposite field, all the boys stood up and cheered. While the boys knew that little fat boy was still the slowest runner on the team, and little skinny boy was still the weakest hitter, that day they showed that they had the guts to hang in, to persevere, to accomplish. At the next game they were picked earlier in the choosing of sides in recognition of their performance.

This masculine trait of performance is inherent in the male, it is not the result of conditioning, and exists in the males of all forms of life. The bulls lead the cows to grazing areas and watering holes, and provide protection against predators such as mountain lions. If the bulls do not do the job well, other bulls take over. If the lion does not adequately protect and provide for his pride, other lions move in. Performance and accomplishment are manifestations of the masculine Gender in all forms of existence.

The female nature however, does not tend towards competition, performance and accomplishment. The female nature is that of giving, nurturing and loving. Is love quantifiable or qualifiable? Can love be measured? A woman's life is one of giving, not just from when she awakens until she sleeps, but 24 hours a day. Does a mother say that she has already loved her children for eight hours and is not interested in overtime? Does a wife say that she loved her husband all week and needs the week end off? A woman's life is a life of unconditional love. It is 100% giving, and is the big draw that a woman has with men, for every man desires at some point to have a respite from the world of competition, a yearning to be loved not for his achievements, but for his being.

A woman wants recognition for her love, and she interprets gifts of flowers, cards, candy, jewelry, a night out, or just words of praise as indications of appreciation and recognition. She does not want to be compared to the performance of other women. She wants to be appreciated by whomever she is trying to please. Aren't most marital arguments aside from a specific crises, based on the wife feeling that she has not been appreciated? Unfortunately she is usually right, for men tend to appreciate their wives in retrospect.

When men are considering leaving an employer, or if they are fired, their talk is of the unreasonableness of the performance standards: that the sales quota was too high, that production costs couldn't be reduced because the union just received a wage increase, that the cost of financing was too high because the company was giving credit terms that were too liberal.

When women are considering leaving an employer, or if they are fired, their talk is of how hard they worked, how much they gave, and that the boss didn't appreciate them.

How then can the female compete in the world of men? She can't. Yes, she can drive a truck, fly a plane, and operate a drill press. But she cannot compete with men, anymore than the cow can compete with the bull or the lioness with the lion.

And who wants this competition? Neither sex. It is the unconditional female love that motivates men to their accomplishments and provides purpose and meaning to their lives. Why should they compete with that entity? And would a woman want to compete with those she loves? For what purpose?

It is the nature of the two Genders to supplement one another, not to compete with one another. Therefore when a woman is put in a situation where she has to compete with men it is unnatural to both sexes, and her survival is dependent on either the love and consideration of the men, or the creation of laws that will inhibit the competitive nature of men.

Regarding the former, when society consisted primarily of hunters, in some tribes only men did the hunting, and in others men and women did the hunting. Tribes in which only men did the hunting eventually survived those in which both sexes did the hunting, because the latter tribes traveled slower.

In our present society we find a similar slow down in the competitive nature of men as women work alongside them. Either the men are being considerate of the women, a practice that slows the men down, or they are being inconsiderate and abusive of the women, which slows everybody down.

To avoid these situations of conflict and to cope with the so called "male prejudice", laws are enacted that strive for "equality " in the workplace. What is equality in the workplace? Is it making the cathode less of a cathode, and the anode less of an anode? Is it suggesting that instead of the electrons speeding from pole to pole, that they sort of mosey along? Whatever the intent of credentialism, the result will be the slowing down of the economic capability of the race, and the concomitant decline of the well being of all the people.

To provide a measurable basis to insure equal opportunity, laws were passed requiring that the same standard be used in evaluating and promoting all people (no room for individual judgment and intuition) especially to minorities like women. Calling a woman a minority is really a twist of logic and definition. There are more women than men, and they own most of the wealth of the nation. Nevertheless, credentials were adopted to make sure that the same standards were used everywhere.

These credentials took the form of high school diplomas, certificates of the completion of courses of study or training, college degrees, test scores, and seniority. We all know that everybody who drives a car has a drivers license, but not everybody who has a license drives well. Every lawyer admitted to the bar is not a good lawyer. Every physician is licensed to practice medicine, but not every physician is a competent doctor. As shown previously, the measure of acceptance by people is performance, but instead of using credentials as a minimum requirement for a position, credentials are being used as a measure of performance of the position. This is especially true in government, academia and large organizations.

In government, civil service exams are given on a frequent basis, the results of which are used to determine promotions and raises. Factors such as tenacity, creativity, daring, determination, and courage do not enter into the evaluation. This hiring and advancement by credentialism creates a bureaucracy that further expands credentialism and imposes this concept upon society, especially upon large corporations. These corporations in turn use credentials in hiring and evaluating in order to not be accused of prejudice by the government.

An effect of credentialism is to exclude from the work force those people who really need the work, and are perhaps motivated, or should be motivated to do the work. Most immigrants in the past who made up the bulk of the poor could not have passed the test of credentialism, They were largely uneducated or poorly educated, but they worked hard and bettered their lot. Today, people in a similar situation are eliminated from a large portion of the job market as a result of credentialism. However, the credentialists will take care of these people by qualifying them for aid in accordance with another set of credentials; the credentials of minimum income, minority status, unwed motherhood, or whatever category the credentialists determine. Credentialism removes people from a productive position in society and places them in a non-productive position. Society loses in several ways. There is the loss of taxes collected from their production, the increase in government expenditure to provide for these people, the loss in national productivity because they are no longer working, and the destruction of the productive and creative will of the recipients.

Many years ago when I started my manufacturing company, there were among my earliest employees two black women from Mississippi. To protect their identities I will refer to them as Bea and Beulah. They were from rural Mississippi had been pregnant at the age of 13 and each had large families. They had been fruit pickers in Florida before coming north to New Jersey. They were both very competent workers and I decided to develop them as best I could. I had them tested for academic ability at a local school that was participating in government activities to help the poor. Bea could read and write at the second grade level, and Beulah could read and write at the fourth grade level. They enrolled in school, received their books and did give continuing their education a try. However, the pressures of family, work, and social environment soon overcame the desire to study, and they dropped out.

They were very proficient at their work and also trustworthy. On days when I had to make customer contact I gave them the keys to the business. They did as much work when I was gone as when I was there. Answering the phone was somewhat of a problem. Beulah who could read and write, could not speak well (she didn't like wearing her false teeth), and Bea who could speak well couldn't read and write very well, so Bea would answer the phone and Beulah would write down the messages.

As business expanded, I hired a secretary, and Bea and Beulah brought in additional workers for the shop, consisting of their friends, relatives and neighbors. Eventually Bea and Beulah became lead persons, and then Bea became my forelady. I was very pleased with the progress that these women had made, and considered myself fortunate to have two such conscientious and loyal workers. That is until the credentialists moved in.

One day Bea informed me that she was getting food stamps. When I asked her why, she explained that some social workers visited her, asked how many children she had and how much she was earning, and determined that she was entitled to food stamps. Shortly thereafter Bea started drinking and her absenteeism increased. By the third month on food stamps she left, and I never saw her again. Beulah told me that she had taken to drinking and had left town.

Beulah was having trouble with varicose veins on her leg, had a couple of operations, and then she too disappeared. I saw her a couple of years later, asked her how she was feeling, and if she cared to come back to work for me. She indicated she was feeling fine, but could I pay her "under the table" because she was on welfare.

The credentialists had taken away from me two dedicated employees, they took out of the work force two producers, they removed from the tax roles two contributors, they increased the tax on society to support these two women, and they turned two hard working honest people into a drunkard and a cheat, respectively. In all probability, these actions contributed to a raise for the credentialists, for their reports indicated how they were able to help two more of society's "under-privileged."

The dual prong of credentialism (credentials to either get a job, or credentials to be compensated for not getting a job) has permeated our society, and has had an inhibiting effect on the progress of all of us, especially the poor. The work ethic is never promulgated, either in film, on TV or in the printed media. What is promulgated is the importance of becoming credentialized. Our high school youth, especially those in poverty areas, are being told of the rewards of an education, how studying computer programing for instance, will put them on the road to financial success. It will not! High school diplomas, college degrees, certificates of completion, and licenses do not get people out of poverty. Hard work and a Will to succeed does. Working longer hours than the next person, doing work the next person doesn't like to do, is what gets people out of poverty. That and the Will, the Will to accomplish, the Will to succeed. the Will to overcome.

However, credentialism has so permeated our thinking, that even those who feel they are not a part of it, are still influenced by it. While writing this article I received a call from a man who said he invented a device that used gravity for its power source. He was an immigrant, and didn't speak English very well. I asked him if he was an engineer. His reply was "No I'm not an engineer, inventions don't come from engineers, they come from God". I had asked for credentials, and the man set me straight, inventions come from the creative WILL, a manifestation of the masculine Gender.

The effects of credentialism are far reaching, and create a loyalty to those who do the credentializing from those who are credentialized. Those who determine eligibility for food stamps and welfare checks have significant power over the recipients, literally the power to control food and lodging. In my business when I had welfare mothers on the payroll, the big competition for their time was always the credentializers. The mothers had to report for physicals, bring the children in for physicals, or report for counseling. As one mother said to me "I take care of first things first, and welfare is first". She knew whom she had to please and whom she didn't have to please. A job was an extracurricular activity; welfare was life itself.

The biggest damage inflicted by the credentializers however, has been upon the young manhood of our nation, upon the potential leaders, creators, producers and protectors of the land. The young males have been kicked out of their homes by a system that rewards women for having children out of wedlock, or at least for not having a man in the house, The system prevents the man from being a husband to the mother of his children or a father to his children. He has been credentialized out of the work force, credentialized out of his home, and not motivated to produce. If he is a welfare child he is raised without being exposed to positive male values, without guidance or direction, and with little opportunity for the expression of his masculinity. If he is not thoroughly beaten, if somehow he holds onto his manhood, his masculine Gender creativity, daring, courage and assertiveness, in what way will he be able to express it?

Suppose he does not have an affinity for sports or an ability for entertainment, (vehicles of self expression which will be covered in subsequent chapters) what then is he to do as a male?

Self-preservation is the primary driving force in our lives; it transcends spirituality and morality. How will this male preserve himself and live out his life with the tools that the creator has given him? Will this young lion join a youth gang and stake out the turf of his group? Will he lay claim to the females in his turf and fend off the advances of the predatory lions of another locale? Will he pursue high-risk high-reward activities such as numbers running, burglary and protection services? Will he go for the jackpot and start dealing in drugs? If he does any of these things what does he have to lose— a life of nothingness? What does he have to gain—a life of somethingness? High risk and high rewards are manifestations of the masculine Gender. Better to die in the pursuit of somethingness than to wallow in the existence of nothingness.

Of course these values will eventually get him apprehended by the law. He will be tried, convicted and put into a cage. The young lions of our society will be swept off the streets and dumped into cages. They may get out, but they will be apprehended again and sent back to the cage. To make sure they don't get out too soon the credentialists will impose harsher penalties, which mean longer terms in cages. The cages are filling up; they are overflowing. To meet this challenge the credentialists will raise taxes so that more cages can be built, so that those who transgress will have a place to go. The streets will be swept clean of the young lions, so long as we have enough cages to put them into.

The way to get control of any grouping of mammals is to remove from the group the dominant males. Some of the more obvious examples are bovines, deer, and horses. Once the bulls, stags and stallions are removed, the herd becomes docile and controllable.

We are in a process of removing the dominant males from our society. We have more than one million men in our jails, and would probably have two million in them if there were enough room. For those who are not in jail, unnatural laws have been enacted such as like work for like pay, equal opportunity hiring, credentials for promotion, the removal of males from the household or diminishing their say in the operation of the household, diminishing their moral influence over their children, and in every way squelching any manifestation of masculinity.

The purpose of this chapter is not to illustrate the effects of this process of emasculation, but to indicate the effects of credentialism on society and how it is taking increasing control of society by the process of emasculation.

There is an aristocracy of credentialists in America that seeks to perpetuate itself at every level. They are the Commissars of America and have affected every aspect of our lives just as the Commissars of Communism effect every aspect of Russian life. We have only to see what it did to them to understand what it is doing to us.

Chaos will always result when society removes the positive manifestation of the masculine Gender.

XVIII
More Thoughts
on Credentialism

One of my earlier observations of the trend toward credentialism and away from performance occurred when I was on active duty with the Navy. Shortly after I assumed the duties of Engineer Officer aboard a destroyer a Chief Machinest Mate had reported aboard for assignment to my department. The service stripes on the sleeves of his uniform were gold instead of red, meaning he had never been subject to disciplinary action for his entire enlistment, which at that time was about 18 years. He had an excellent record, was courteous, correct, and as I was soon to learn, incompetent. The men did not obey him, they laughed at him and ridiculed him. He could not lead or maintain discipline. When it came time to prepare his semi-annual performance report I indicated these shortcomings.

Headquarters returned the report to me, as it was considered to be a negative report on an otherwise excellent record, and more substantiation of this negative assessment was required. In reviewing the Chief's record the reason for the seemingly inconsistent evaluation became apparent. His previous assignment was at a Naval Supply depot. Prior to that he was an instructor. Prior to that he had been in school. He had never had sea duty as a Chief, and very little leadership experience ashore. He had a lot of credentials, but very little in the way of accomplishment. What was needed aboard ship was a man who was tenacious, could inspire a following, and could get the job done. These are the requirements of combat leadership, and being aboard ship was training for combat. Credentials weren't going to win any battles or save any lives. I stuck with the evaluation made in my report, and it was accepted.

At that time I noticed a preference on the part of younger officers for staff rather than line positions. They preferred positions in Washington, with Naval Intelligence or Ordinance, positions offering high visibility and requiring and creating lots of credentialism. This decline in the regard for line officers by the new intelligentsia is described in the novel *"The Caine Mutiny"*, when Lt. Tom Keefer tells Ensign Willie Kieth that the ship's engine room is a place "designed by geniuses to be run by idiots". Lt. Keefer was a line officer, but he expressed the growing contempt of the military intelligentsia for line officers.

The names of military heroes remembered by the general public are the names of line officers: Admiral Arleigh "30 knot" Burke of the Navy, General "Chesty" Puller of the Marine Corps, and General George S. Patton of the Army. They were not known for their credentials, they were known for their performance. They earned the little tin medals of recognition of their peer group: The Distinguished Service Cross, The Medal of Honor, The Silver Star, The Bronze Star and the Purple Heart. They won battles; they got the job done. They performed.

In government, the trend to staff rather than line was exemplified in the composition of the Kennedy cabinet, which is well described by David Halberstam in his book *"The Best and the Brightest"*. An excerpt from this book recounting Johnson's awe of the Kennedy cabinet follows: Stunned by their glamour and intellect, he (Johnson) rushed back to tell Rayburn, his great and crafty mentor, about them, about how brilliant each was, that fellow Bundy from Harvard, Rusk from Rockefeller, McNamara from Ford. On he went, naming them all. "Well, Lyndon, you may be right and they may be every bit as intelligent as you say," said Rayburn, "but I'd feel a whole lot better about them if just one of them had run for sheriff once."

Rayburn would have liked to see line officers in the cabinet, people who had been on the front lines, who had been in touch with the public. Rayburn and Johnson were line officers in the field of government, the Kennedy cabinet members were all staff, and even their wartime duties were staff duties. They were the credentialists of government.

With a staff government out of touch with its people, and a staff military out of touch with its combat personnel, is it any wonder that Vietnam was a disaster? The decisiveness, courage and determination of the masculine Gender was missing. Depending upon one's political persuasion, Vietnam was either something to get into completely, or stay out of entirely. Women and children go wading, men sit on the beach or go swimming. We went wading in Vietnam, and almost drowned as a nation.

The trend from line to staff, from performance to credentialism began to permeate the business world as well with the advent and then proliferation of the MBA. The original concept for their existence was a good one: a degree in one discipline coupled with a Masters in business administration, enabling the individual to translate the developments of engineering, manufacturing, and sales, into profits. However these MBA's did not want to be in engineering, manufacturing or sales, they wanted staff positions in finance, marketing, and corporate planning. They did not want to be out in the field, or on the firing line of the production floor. They did not feel the need to prove themselves to their peer group, they felt that with the MBA they had already earned the recognition they needed. Eventually they did not even want to join manufacturing companies at all, opting instead for positions with consulting firms, investment bankers, brokerage firms, banks, and other financial institutions. Rather than being involved in the creation of wealth, then chose instead to be in the administration and distribution of it.

Those firms, usually the largest corporations, that hired a proliferation of MBA's and assorted staff people, began to change their emphasis from innovation and the development of new markets, products and services, to internal efficiencies such as cost reduction and control, budgeting, reduced expenditures (which frequently meant reductions in amounts spent on R & D, and new product development), and corporate planning. These efficiencies, and controls, were for the most part needed by all of American industry. However, no matter how much expenses are reduced, it is income that generates profits, and very little emphasis was placed on future income. The planning was all short term, it was on the utilization of wealth, rather than the creation of wealth.

The influence of staff activities eventually reached smaller firms, the entrepreneurial establishments that depended upon the daring, courageous, tenacious manifestations of the masculine Gender. These firms could not normally afford staff personnel of any ilk, but their services were made possible by the constantly proliferating consulting firms. Staffed with people who had not succeeded on the firing line, or perhaps were never on it, but who were considerably credentialized, these firms were now convincing the entrepreneurs, those people who were always on the firing line, that their businesses would benefit from the planning, organizational structure and staff procedures that were made available to them on a per diem basis.

One such entrepreneurial firm was a customer of mine. The owner, Marvin, was a stereotype of the top of the head, shirtsleeve management of small firms. He worked 12 hour days six days a week, carried the inventory around in his head, along with the pricing and purchasing. He made a decent living in a competitive market.

When his father-in-law died, his wife Sarah inherited a fair amount of money and decided to invest some of it in Marvin's business. The investment she made entitled her to a majority stock position, so while Marvin remained as President, Sarah became the Chairman of the Board.

Sarah's objective was to get Marvin out of the 12 hour day, six day a week routine, and into a more relaxed and pleasant mode of living. She hired a well known consulting firm, and for $75,000 they analyzed the company, determined its growth potential, created a management structure for attaining that potential, prepared organization charts, and trained Sarah and Marvin in the art of delegating authority.

Marvin stopped coming in at 6AM and going home at 6PM. Now he and Sarah came in at 9 and went home at 3. No more musty old pants and rolled up shirtsleeves for Marvin, he now wore expensive clothes and they stayed un-rumpled. The metamorphosis of Marvin was amazing. He used to talk so fast that he almost stuttered. He used to zip around the office and shop in such a flurry that caused everyone to become nervous. Now he was relaxed and congenial.

Marvin and Sarah did delegate a lot, just as they had been taught. They went to trade shows, read trade publications and attended seminars. They did what the consultants told them that top management should do, delegate what could be delegated and spend time on what couldn't be.

The business did well for a while, but when the general business climate declined, the situation at Marvin's place deteriorated rapidly. Sales dropped, profits dwindled, overhead increased in relation to sales, customers were lost, and suppliers weren't being paid. Bankruptcy was looming on the horizon. Sarah said, "Marvin do something". And Marvin did something.

He came to work at 6AM in old clothes and stayed until he was ready to drop from fatigue. He took the organization charts off the wall, and threw them away along with the business plan. He made aggressive sales calls, slashed overhead, and made all the major decisions and most of the minor ones. Marvin regained control of his company and returned it to a profitable basis.

The lesson to be learned is that there must be a balance in the manifestation of Gender in business as in all else in the universe. Sarah's intentions were good, even noble, for she wanted a better life for her husband and herself. The consulting firm was probably also well intentioned, as Marvin's business could have benefited from some staff input. However, what had happened was that Marvin had been temporarily emasculated. The control of the company had been taken away from him, stripping him of any authority with which to implement the positive manifestations of the masculine Gender. The activities of the company were involved in nurturing the results of the past, not the creativity of the future. Eventually there would be nothing to nurture. Fortunately Marvin regained his manhood in time to save the company. Large corporations are not saved as easily.

Larger business concerns can not readily hire a large group of bulls or lions to make up for the lack of creative, pioneering manifestation of the masculine Gender that plagues them. In fact, they do not recognize what is plaguing them. Instead, they proceed along increasingly staff-oriented activities, reducing costs, eliminating product lines, spinning off divisions, merging with other firms, becoming available for take over, and going into bankruptcy, all rear guard actions that do not generate anything. For a business to survive, it must not only be efficient, but aggressive as well. Line activities provide that aggressiveness. Staff activities support it.

Another major area of credentialism is within our educational institutions. This is somewhat natural since we like to have our places of learning accredited. Part of the process of accreditation is a review of the credentials of the faculty. How many and what kinds of degrees they have, how many papers they have written, how many books they have published, how many articles they have authored, how many societies, organizations, and clubs they belong to, are all considered in evaluating the faculty and determining the accreditation of the institution. This appears to be a reasonable, fair and just approach. However, on closer examination, it will prove to be a superficial approach that inhibits the fulfilling of the objective of the institution.

The objective of schools and universities is not the storing of knowledge; we have libraries for that purpose. The objective is to impart knowledge from those who have it to those who seek it. The academic standing of these institutions should be judged by the knowledge they impart, as well as the knowledge they contain.

To have professors write papers that only their contemporaries in other universities read, to attend symposiums of their colleagues, to author articles for magazines that only their peers read, and to have degrees in disciplines that they do not teach, are activities that promote self-aggrandizement, not the transferring of knowledge from those who have it to those who seek it.

Some of the finest classroom instructors, whether they are high school teachers or college professors, are those with the minimum credentials necessary for their position. Frequently they do not have the opportunity to get advanced degrees because of the limitations of time or income. Sometimes it's just because they love their work and they spend their free time devising different methods of imparting knowledge to their students. These men and women instructors in the classrooms are the line officers of education. They are on the firing line. They are not dealing with abstractions, they are dealing with the reality of the educational process. The quality of instruction that these people give is a lot more important than any student teacher ratios. Any true educational innovations will come from their input. Yet these very people are the ones being by-passed for promotion because of their lack of credentials. Therefore, the policies, and curriculum are increasingly being made and planned by those least aware of the requirements of the instructors and students. This is resulting in an educational system that is stagnating, that is fostering credentialism rather than promoting accomplishment. It is turning academia into tired old institutions with little vitality with which to innovate.

There must be a balance between line and staff in every organization, just as there must be a balance between the masculine and feminine Genders throughout the universe. If an organization is excessively line oriented it will collapse internally, as almost happened with Ford Motor Company because of Henry Ford's disdain for staff people, people whom he referred to as "non-productive workers" and whom he fired at whim. The major problem facing organizations and businesses today is not the lack of support staff, it is the lack of creative Will, of pioneering spirit that brings about innovation and creates new wealth. An example of the lack of this creative will in an entire industry, and its resultant decline is in the field of transportation, and will be the subject of the next chapter.

XIX
The Rise & Fall of Our Transportation Industry

The industry most identified with the growth of America, possibly the raison d'etre for America, is transportation. From the British desire to retain the colonies for the large virgin forests which would be a source of masts for their merchant and naval fleet, to the advent of clipper ships that would set speed records that would not be broken until after World War II, to the invention of the steamboat that would ply the coastal waters, to the riverboats that would navigate the inland waters, to the covered wagon, stage coach, and railroad that would interconnect the nation, to the automobile, truck and plane, that would integrate it, America has been engrossed with, enraptured by, and involved in the development of the transportation industry.

All of the positive manifestations of masculine Gender were brought into play in the evolvement of the transportation industry: The conceptual thinking that caused the invention and/or development of the clipper ship, steamboat, automobile, truck and airplane, and the courage, determination and raw strength needed to cross mountains, unfurl sails in heavy winds, and lay thousands of miles of track by hand; the faith that caused men to invest heretofore unheard of sums of money that would not be repaid until the railroad or ship was built and carrying cargo; the pioneering spirit that developed wagon trains, refrigerated cargoes, and airmail; and the inventiveness that developed new materials, new fuels, new roads.

Romance was in the air. What woman did not dream of being married to a Clipper Ship or Riverboat captain, a pilot with his goggles and silk scarf, a wagon train master, or even just a laborer who was working on the railroad? Working on the railroad, oh what that phrase conjured up in the minds of people; working on the new, the daring, the innovative, the powerful.

The innovations caused by transportation created whole new support industries: the demand for coal, oil, rubber, iron, steel, asphalt, concrete, batteries, and glass created huge new industrial giants. Almost everything produced in America was used by the transportation industry. Powerful men created powerful companies which spawned powerful unions. Every American was touched in one way or another by the growth of this all pervasive industry. We are so romanticized by this industry that movies about the horse culture, railroads, ships, and aviation, still draw large audiences.

The transportation industry started to decline at the beginning of the last half of this century, and its decline is representative of the decline of any industry in which the positive application of masculine Gender has decreased. At the end of World War II half of the world's maritime tonnage was American. Almost half of all the merchant ships in the world were sailing under the American flag. There were huge shipping companies such as U.S. Lines, American Export Lines, Grace Lines, Lykes Brothers Steamship, American President Lines, and Isbrandsten Steamship. Powerful unions such as the NMU, SIU, MEBA, MM&P and ILA represented the men and women aboard these ships, and those that loaded their cargoes. By 1965 most of these fleets had vanished, and the unions were but shells of their former selves. But this is getting ahead of the story, for America's romance with its merchant fleet had ended a century earlier.

The end of the era of Clipper Ships coincided with the end of the Civil War and the beginning of the opening of the West. When the American frontier reached the Pacific, and East and West were tied together by the railroads, America's gaze turned inward, and would remain that way until the latter part of the 20th Century. The first 13 States admitted to the Union all had coastlines whereas, only nine of the next 35 would have coastlines. When an American saw a railroad train, or an airplane, he or she knew that wherever that plane or train came from, or would go to, it would be in America. To most Americans, the world was America—there was no need to look outward.

Therefore, the large American merchant fleet of post World War II was an aberration, the second maritime aberration of the century, the first being the building of a huge merchant fleet during World War I. This second aberration was primarily a fleet of stepchildren, by-products of the huge manufacturing capacity of America, rather than of an American interest in commerce or the sea. The American Shipping industry suffered not only from a lack of the manifestation of masculine Gender, but from the lack of the manifestation of feminine Gender as well. It became a manifestation of neuter Gender, much like a steer that is led off to slaughter. It was natural then that those who had an interest in shipping and commerce—the Scandinavians and Greeks—would adopt the orphaned American shipping industry; they would exhibit the masculine Gender necessary to develop large viable merchant fleets. Hardly a tear was shed for the loss of these stepchildren, for how many Americans even knew what the Merchant Marine was?

Every American, however, knew what the railroads were. The names of the railroads became household knowledge: The Baltimore and Ohio, Chicago Northwestern, Louisville and Nashville, The Santa Fe, and the mighty Penn Central were known by most people. These were not just companies to go to work for, they were organizations to be identified with. Working for the railroad was more than a job, it was participating in the making of history. Fighting the elements, fighting the terrain, pushing to the limits of human endurance, innovating, gambling, organizing, leading, motivating, were all a part of being associated with the railroads. However, once the last track was laid, and the last spike driven into the tie, it was as if the last positive manifestation of masculine Gender went in with it. And therein began the demise of the railroads.

The railroads ceased to be innovative, daring, and aggressive. It could be said that they were affected to some degree by credentialism, but most of it was from without rather than within. The regulation of the railroads included the requirement of running unprofitable routes in order to be allowed to have profitable routes-pure socialism. The legalizing of the practice of featherbedding by the unions added to the socialism. Various other governmental regulations at the federal, state and local levels would also inhibit the efficient operation of the railroads. However, these activities were but vehicles for the demise of that which had already been abandoned.

And indeed the railroads had been abandoned. They became devoid of the positive manifestations of both masculine and feminine Genders, and suffered as a result of one of the most negative manifestations of masculine Gender—slothfulness.

It is male slothfulness that dissipates the wealth of rich families and reduces them to poverty, and it is male slothfulness that keeps those in poverty from rising out of it. It is male slothfulness that breaks down the family, tribe and race. It is male slothfulness that destroys organizations. The management of the railroads became slothful, and the industry deteriorated as a result.

When the railroads had finished laying their track, they had no competition. As was mentioned earlier, men are recognized by their peer group for their performance. If there is no peer group, there is no standard to measure performance against. Consequently performance deteriorates, and at some point it becomes slothful. Railroad management had non-competitive peer groups. Their association with each other was more in the vein of contemporaries, and at their various club meetings they could discuss how they were divvying up the transportation market between them. Government regulation and union demands could be easily tolerated, as increased costs could be readily transferred to their customers. The operation of the railroads became a socialistic partnership consisting of the government, unions and rail operators. Socialism stifles initiative and fosters slothfulness, whether in be in the form of welfare, food stamps, government subsidies to business or exclusive franchises. Slothfulness does not lead to innovation and improvement. Instead it causes deterioration and obsolescence.

When trucking was finally recognized as competition by the railroads, the railroads did make some innovations such as piggy back transportation (carrying loaded trailers on flatbed cars) and rent-a- train arrangements for large customers, but these responses came after the competitive inroads made by trucking were irreversible. The railroads never did seriously look upon the airlines as competition. In fact, they were relieved that they could reduce their own passenger operations. The railroads entered a period of demise as a result of the negative manifestation of the masculine Gender—slothfulness.

The fate that befell the railroads very nearly befell the automobile companies as well. The pent-up domestic and world-wide demand for automobiles after World War II, coupled with America being the almost exclusive source of automobiles, resulted in an essentially non-competitive relationship amongst the American automobile companies. They produced as many cars as possible, as fast as possible for as high a price as possible. Management efforts were directed towards satisfying what was for a while an insatiable demand for cars. Market research, customer preferences, new innovations were not high priority concerns. Detroit was manufacturing cars designed according to what they decided was best for the consumer.

In 1953 a small unattractive automobile with an air-cooled engine and very few amenities was introduced to America. It was called the Volkswagen and was met with derision by the automobile companies. The sales of the Volkswagen to the American market increased substantially from year to year for 16 consecutive years. During this period the automobile companies repeatedly told Americans that they did not want a small car. Our merchant fleet deteriorated because of disinterest, and our railroads because of slothfulness, if our automobile companies were to fail, it would be because of arrogance—another negative manifestation of masculine Gender.

The arrogance of the automobile companies was not without its support, or at least its acknowledgement. In his book "The New Industrial State", John Kenneth Galbraith, the renowned economic credentialist stated that General Motors could build a car of any design and sell it, that GM was above the demands of the market. He also stated that the Fortune 500 do not go broke either. It would be interesting to review the 1967 and 1990 Fortune 500 lists, and then have Mr. Galbraith enlighten us as to the reason for the disappearance of so many of the names on the 1967 list. Mr. Galbraith also indicated that Ford Motor Company was having difficulties because it had grown larger than what Mr. Ford could control, that he did not understand that modern business had to be run by technocrats. So much for the thinking of economic credentialism. The fact is that in a free market General Motors and any other company, had to provide the product and/or services that the public wanted, or run the risk of going out of business. No amount of propaganda could change this fact; at best it could only delay its reality. Technocrats do not run businesses anymore than a cook runs a restaurant, or a roughneck runs an oil company. If corporations do not stay alert to the demands of the market, if they do not invest in fundamental and applied research, if they do not provide the leadership necessary to highly motivate their people, then they are not exhibiting the positive manifestations of the masculine Gender, and they will eventually fail. Technocrats, credentialists, and socialists are not the causes of failure; they are evidences of the lack of positive manifestations of masculine Gender at the helm of the organization, which in turn will lead to failure.

The American automobile companies were fortunate in that foreign competition increased, first from Europe and then from Japan, creating a competitive peer group that would attract a positive manifestation of the masculine Gender. Management stopped making pronouncements about what the people wanted, and began listening to the people to learn what they wanted. New styling was introduced, cars were made smaller, more fuel efficient, and safer. Old plants were closed and new plants were built, new production methods were experimented with, and union cooperation was elicited to lower costs and improve productivity. Dynamic sales campaigns were conducted, and creative financing was introduced. American automobile companies began to exhibit vitality—they were once again being managed by a positive manifestation of the masculine Gender. All this was accomplished without import restrictions, government subsidies, and credentialist advice. How long the American automobile companies remain viable entities is dependent upon how long they exercise the positive manifestations of masculine Gender.

This improvement in performance of the American automobile companies was a relative one, the performance became a lot better than it had been, but was not close to what could be attained. A recent example of further improvements is the performance of Detroit Diesel Corp, a manufacturer of truck engines. Owned by General Motors Corp, it accounted for only 3.2% of the truck engine market in 1987. Roger Penske bought control of Detroit Diesel Corp. in 1988, and immediately thereafter the positive manifestations of the masculine Gender were applied to its operation. More than 20% of the salaried jobs were eliminated, leadership was shown in the improved relationship between management and labor, an aggressive sales program was implemented, innovations were fostered resulting in the first methanol-fueled heavy engine to meet California and federal clean air standards. By the first half of 1991 Detroit Diesel's market share increased to 23%, a remarkable achievement in a very short period of time.

The market had not changed, the product had not changed, what had changed was the management of the company. It went from a staff oriented, credentially loaded operation, to a line oriented aggressive operation. When there is a manifestation of the positive aspects of the masculine Gender any organization will succeed. Products might become obsolete, markets might become saturated, but virile management will always lead the organization to new and successful ventures.

The trucking industry became deregulated during the Reagan administration, and shippers benefited immediately. Freight rates decreased, and innovative services were offered to the shippers. The truckers of course did not feel that deregulation was beneficial in that profits declined and many companies went out of business, including such giants as Associated Transport and TIME-DC. The failure of various enterprises usually occurs in the early stages of competition, a modern day example of the survival of the fittest. However, those that survive are better able to supply the market with what it needs, thus making the entire market more viable. Deregulation was in essence decreasing the influence of the credentialists in the trucking industry, permitting a more dynamic management approach. The industry still has not seen the creativity and pioneering spirit necessary for significant innovations, but it nevertheless has become more aggressive and performance oriented.

The airline industry is also going through the throes of a competitive shakeout which is causing the disappearance of some of the major carriers. This process has provided all sorts of benefits to the passengers, primarily in the area of lower fares, and like trucking, the industry has become more aggressive in its sales approach. Nevertheless, the attitude of the airline industry, like all the other segments of the transportation industry, regardless of some sporadic vitality, is one of passivity.

There appears to be a pervasive feeling that all the tracks have been laid and the stations built, all the planes have been manufactured and the terminals erected, all the trucks and cars have been designed and the roads constructed, that there is little more that can be developed. If that is the thinking, then it is a certainty that the transportation industry will decline.

However, if a renewed manifestation of masculine Gender is applied to the various components of the transportation industry, it will once again, invent, innovate, create and expand. Recent developments in cryogenics and superconductors will make possible the building of trains that can average 300 miles per hour. That would be four hours from New York to Chicago allowing for a few stops. Air transportation is now four hours, two on the plane, and two going to and from the airport. There would be no problems due to inclement weather or heavy traffic. That would also mean four hour trips from New York to Miami. The railroads could build multi level parking garages over their stations to allow for easy access to the train, and ticket-operated vending machines offering one free sandwich to the traveler, or credit card operated gourmet machines, and free coffee. Wouldn't that be a move ahead in transportation? Electric cars are going to be introduced by the Japanese next year. Europe already has electric buses. Is there a viable market for solar operated transportation? Can the hover craft principle (fans blowing air downward keeping the vehicle slightly off the ground) be applied commercially to cars? These are just a few of the innovations that are available now, and there must be many other creative possibilities that will come to the fore with the proper management at the helm.

The lethargy that we have seen in our major industry is indicative of the lethargy that exists throughout all of the major business concerns in America. Even those that are facing stiff competition are fighting a rear-guard action with improved efficiencies and reduced expenditures. These activities can delay failure, but the true antidotes are creativity, a pioneering spirit, determination and will, all positive manifestations of the masculine Gender.

XX
Still More Thoughts on Credentialism

During the time that I wrote this book, I contacted a literary agent in the neighborhood to ask her opinion of what I had written. Her immediate response was "what are your credentials?"

She wanted to know if I had a degree in social work or psychology, if I was on the lecture circuit, if I had been on a talk show on TV or radio, or if I had any other credentials that would justify writing a book about society. If not, she then advised that since I had no credentials, I should forget about getting the book published. If there was any one event that enforced my Will to get this book published, that was it

Who am I, a man without credentials, to consider writing a book about my brothers and sisters in life? Do I need credentials to observe, to experience, to reflect, to give and receive, to love and be loved, to care, to empathize, to learn, to grow, to contribute, to create, to be? I have traveled the land and sailed the oceans of this earth, and have walked and talked with, dined with, and pressed my flesh against members of royalty, government and the peasantry of four continents; I have laughed with, cried with, danced with, and lain with those of every color; I have ridden on planes, trains, buses, ships, ferries and subways, and have listened to my brothers and sisters who sat down beside me and told me of their fears, frustrations, hurts, anxieties, loves, misfortunes, and illnesses; I have sat on park benches, in waiting rooms, in bars, in restaurants, and had my brothers and sisters share with me, and advise me, and give to me. Am I not capable of developing wisdom from all that I have seen and done? Is it not my obligation to share this wisdom with my brothers and sisters? Who shall bestow authority upon me, and make me worthy of speaking and writing and sharing with my brothers and sisters? Am I not self worthy? Are not my life's experiences such that others can learn from them, as I have learned from others? Yet, I have no credentials.

I was born of European parents, one from the Mediterranean and one from north Europe, and was exposed to two cultures, languages and religions. Born poor, I spent a childhood in the depression years, had the good fortune to rise up economically and have a large home in the suburbs, a summer home, and two cars. A product of city, state and federal school systems, I had the opportunity to obtain a superior education. Yet, I have no credentials.

I served on active duty with the Navy as an officer and experienced the rigors of training, the hazards of sea duty, and witnessed the homesickness of married men for their wives and children. I took to myself a wife, had four children - two boys and two girls, and experienced the joy of parenthood and all its myriad responsibilities. I also experienced the trauma of divorce, of seeing all that I had lived for dispersed and almost cease to exist; and of seeing my children hurt, confused and angry. I have seen others lose their children to drugs, alcohol and waywardness. I have heard the travail of women who told me they lay awake in bed at night wondering if they had been good mothers and wives. Yet, I have no credentials.

I was an active member of my church, served on every committee, taught church school and gave sermons. I read the bible, Bhagavad-Gita, the Upanishads, the Tao, excerpts from the teachings of Mohammed and the Buddha, and studied a wide range of the Yoga philosophy. I read Plato, Epicurus, Dantes, Cervantes and Whitman. Yet, I have no credentials.

I started a business from nothing, built it up to a 20,000-square foot manufacturing facility, and supported a family of six from the profits. I also lost everything I had and am now in the process of building a new business and a new life. I traveled through most of the States calling on every major industry in America, visiting assembly lines, job shops, breweries and construction sites. Yet, I have no credentials.

I was on the leading edge of what is now considered to be new-age knowledge, involved in handwriting analysis, numerology, astrology, psychic phenomena, reflexology, and holistic medicine before they became popular. Yet, I have no credentials.

I am 62 years old and am in the same situation as the youth who does not have a high school diploma. We have no credentials and are either unemployable or under-employable. Our best chance for success is to independently use our own ingenuity. We have been asked for our credentials, but no one has asked if we are industrious, reliable, creative, punctual and honest. We have not been asked what we have done, what we can do, or what we can contribute. I can empathize with that youth and the millions of men across this country who have been, and are being denied opportunity because they do not have the credentials. Yet, I too have no credentials.

I see the injustice that has been and continues to be created by weak-kneed milksop government officials who create laws emasculating men, and the devastation the it wreaks upon society. Yet, I have no credentials.

I know that it is time for change, that the deterioration of the race must stop, that a realization of our true purpose and the means to attain it must take place. I know that what is propounded in this book is right, and that this book will be published. Yet, I have no credentials.

XXI
Opportunities for the Non-Credentialized Male

The effect of credentialism has been to reduce the opportunities for men to manifest the positive aspects of the masculine Gender, especially those men who are at the poverty level. If their manliness has not been snuffed out entirely, there will be a natural, instinctive, self-preservative effort of the will by these males, to seek out areas of opportunity in which to manifest the characteristics of the masculine Gender.

One of the least credentialized areas of potential income is in the domain of sports. Sports, especially athletics, provides the opportunity for males without credentials to express the attributes of their masculine Gender, and is the reason that athletics at any given time tends to be most influenced by the particular ethnic or racial group that is at the bottom of the economic ladder. This is especially so in boxing, a sport that is extremely brutal and dangerous, and appeals only to those who cannot earn a decent living elsewhere.

Another area of opportunity for the poor without credentials is the entertainment industry, especially the music segment. Like athletics, success in entertainment is predicated upon performance, a natural activity of the masculine Gender. There are very few credentials required in the music industry, especially in popular music.

Just prior to, and immediately following World War II, there was a strong Italian-American influence in sports and entertainment. They were the second largest immigrant group to come to this country between the two World Wars, and as such were starting at the bottom of the economic ladder. Names such as Rocky Graziano, Carmine Bascillio, Jake LaMatta and Rocky Marciano dominated boxing. In baseball there were the legendary DiMaggio brothers, Frankie Crossetti, Phil Rizzuto, Ernie Lombardi, Carl Furillo and Tony Cuccinello. In music there was Frank Sinatra, Louis Prima, Perry Como and Julius LaRosa. As the economic lot of Italian-Americans improved, they began to have less of an influence in athletics and music and more of an influence in business and politics.

This is not to say that success in athletics or entertainment per se, will cause a given group to rise out of poverty, it is however, indicative of the opportunities that a poverty group will utilize to improve their economic situation. They will do the most difficult tasks, and work longer hours for less pay than others of a higher economic strata. Each new immigrant poverty group made its imprint on society: Italians; shoe repair shops, produce stands and barber shops, Greeks; luncheonettes, and floral shops, Germans; meat markets, machine shops and dance halls, Jews; retail stores, Irish; taverns, Chinese; hand laundries, Koreans; convenience markets, and Indians magazine stands. All these enterprises involved long hours, frequently on the part of the entire family, and many times with minimal return until the business was accepted and utilized by the consumer.

Athletics and entertainment still offer opportunity to the uncredentialized male, but unlike his predecessors who had a strong familial and tribal support structure to operate from, the male who is functioning at the poverty level today is essentially alone. More than likely raised without a male role model, not having a familial or tribal support structure, he is left to fend for himself. If he does not adapt to his environment, he is swept off the streets and into jail.

The government of the past 30 years has enacted laws that have broken down the familial structure, emasculated men, and credentialized away opportunities for advancement. The male who is in poverty today is increasingly alone, and his chances of working his way out of poverty are diminishing. The poor of our nation are increasingly becoming wards of the State, which is a modern political expression meaning slaves.

The longer that we let this trend continue the more difficult it will be to correct it. The time for change is now, and that change must be a reassertion of the masculine Gender, a taking back control of our lives from the government, and making the government our servant instead of our master.

XXII
The Demise of
American Unions

American unions have improved working conditions for every American and for most people throughout the world. They have created respect for the worker, dignity in the workplace, and civility in interactions with management. American Unions are also in their death throes.

The union movement came into being at a time of intense economic activity and industrialization. Men left their homes and went to the mines, the wilderness, the deserts, the factories; to dig for coal, lay track, drill for oil and produce automobiles, and worked long hours in an almost inhuman environment. The nation was adjusting to the results of an outpouring of male technological creativity never before seen. To build these new products and the necessary supporting structure required economic and social relationships that were without precedent. Much as industry was blazing new trails in the production of goods and services, the unions were blazing new trails in the relationship of workers to their environment and their employers.

The employers considered this activity on the part of their employees as an infringement of their management function, and for the most part resisted all attempts at unionization of the work force. Once the work force was unionized, every concession to labor had to be almost literally wrested from the grip of management. There was intense conflict between these two groups: the one having an heretofore unheard of concentration of capital, and the other an heretofore unheard of concentration of labor. The relationship between management and labor was extremely adversarial, but both groups were pioneers, and collectively they ushered in a new era in transportation, production, communication and entertainment. One group was continually creating new products and methods of producing them, while the other group was creating new ways for workers to cope with this change. Each group was courageous, daring, adventurous, forceful and uncompromising in their goals.

Most of what the unions fought for is now law. The forty-hour work week, unemployment compensation, workers compensation, temporary disability, minimum wage, and child labor laws, were all pioneered by the unions. Their efforts were resisted not only by management, but frequently by the government and general public. The unions persevered, and many times their members endured personal injury and imprisonment in their efforts to accomplish their goals. Eventually they were accepted by the public, supported by the government, and recognized by all as the chosen representatives of the workers.

If there was one negative effect that unions had on the economy, and on the general feeling of the populace towards the unions, it was the obtaining of wages above what the normal free market would dictate. To obtain a raise for no other reason than the employer's desire to avoid a strike has a negative effect on the economy. To strike for these ends produced negative feelings among the American public, and even a sense of a lack of fair play amongst many union members themselves. When I first started my business I had a part-time secretary who had worked for Railway Express, and whose husband still did. She told me the wages they received for the work they did was so high that she felt it was sinful. Eventually this condition of overpaid workers corrected itself as Railway Express went bankrupt and the Union's members lost thousands of jobs.

Constraints of the free market system will always produce a negative result, and wage increases received for no reason other than the power of the union to strike are such a constraint. The general public tends to support a strike that it perceives to be for legitimate reasons; it however, resents being inconvenienced by a strike the success of which will mean higher costs to themselves. The ultimate result of increased wages for other than economic reasons is Socialism.

Another area of public discontent with unions is the unionization of government employees. We have a democratic form of government, or more properly, a representative form of government, and expect that our representatives will be answerable to us for whatever actions they take. When government employees are unionized, the decisions of our representatives frequently are based on their relationship with the unions, rather than on their relationship with the electorate. There is a growing resentment to this divided loyalty, and as the economy lags, this resentment will translate into actions against the unions, especially in strongly unionized cities such as New York.

Unions prospered when industry prospered, when there was a free expression of masculine creativity and the implementation of the creative Will. As this manifestation of masculine Gender decreased, industry began to be less virile and creative, and less expansion oriented. Growth became a result of acquisition and merger, rather than new product development and increased demand. Profits became more a function of cost cutting rather than revenue generating. There is a limit as to how much costs can be cut, and a point at which revenues must be increased. If companies are not able to generate sufficient revenues, they deteriorate and then go out of business. When the manifestation of the creative will of the masculine Gender is curtailed, economic decline and the resultant chaos are always the net result. This same malaise has infected the unions, who no longer pioneer, but like the large corporations, administrate instead.

The unions can decide that they have fulfilled their reason for being, and disband. Or they can devote their energies to less masculine activities, such as drawing their power from the government instead of the economy, or focusing their attention on keeping the washrooms clean. Or they can realize that progress can come only from a strong manifestation of masculine Gender, and that it serves the union's best interests to foster and promote the very power that caused their coming into existence.

Union's can only prosper in a healthy growing economy. A healthy growing economy can only occur if there is an unimpeded manifestation of the masculine Gender. For the Unions to survive, they have but one option, and that is to promote a free economy. That means no government hiring standards, no equal pay for equal work philosophy, no unnecessary credentialism, no lobbying to preserve large impotent businesses, and no resisting of labor-saving devices. It means promoting and fostering new areas of development and growth. We will eventually be working and producing in outer space. What are the hazards of working out there? What special considerations are required for the benefit of the workers? The exploration and colonization of space can open up new frontiers for unions, as can the development of undersea activities. More important, the environment for entrepreneurial activity must be improved, even though small businesses do not provide a fertile ground for unionization, the small businesses that develop successful new products create new industries that can offer great potential for unionization.

The unions can either promote free enterprise, and grow and prosper accordingly, or, like the large corporations that have run out of masculine virility, they can start preparations for their own demise.

XXIII
It's New

New is the magic word in advertising. New cars, restaurants, hotels, computers, and telephones are some of the many products continually advertised in all the media. Even if it is a basic product that is not new such as detergent or aspirin, it is advertised as "new and improved". We Americans are captivated by the word new. We want to go to new places and try new things, start a new job, buy new clothes, live in a new home. Our penchant for new has been criticized, joked about, ridiculed, and cited as a flaw in the American character.

What is not generally realized is that NEW is responsible for our life of abundance. NEW has been responsible for the products and services necessary to nurture our society during its tremendous growth in population. NEW is the result of the free expression of the creative Will of the masculine Gender.

The economic collapse that led to the dissolution of the Soviet Union was not a result of totalitarianism,; it was a consequence of the constrained creative Will. Nazi Germany had a totalitarian government, but it produced the hydrogen submarine, rocketry, and the "heavy water" concept of atomic power. Some will say that these developments were a product of the industrious German character, but if that were the case, what happened to the industrious German character in East Germany? East Germany and the Soviet Union had one thing in common, not language, not culture, not religion, but an economic system that constrained the natural creative Will of the masculine Gender. There was no NEW in the Soviet Union or Eastern Europe.

For all the talk and finger pointing about how women participated in all aspects of the Communist economy, how they were in the factories and farms, in the administration, in medicine and the universities, there was never the realization that these women were not doing anything NEW. They were employed by a society that did not know the source of NEW, and consequently had very little NEW. Manufacturing plants in the Eastern block nations and the Soviet Union were like well kept museums, what was once NEW was preserved to look like NEW, but it couldn't function as NEW.

An attitude has developed in this country that women are no longer dependent upon men for their material necessities as was say, a Watusi wife, who depended upon her husband to hunt the lion, or an American Indian squaw who depended upon her husband to hunt a buffalo. The modern American woman is no longer directly dependent on men for her sustenance. She can drive trucks, fly planes, work on assembly lines, construct buildings, and operate computers. She can study engineering, science, medicine, accounting and the law. She is independent in the economic and political sense. That's what women in the Communist countries also thought about their situation.

What both Communist and American women fail to realize is that every thing that they touch, from when they awake in the morning until they retire at night was invented, designed and produced by a man. The alarm clock, toaster, telephone, hair curler, automobile, typewriter, computer, electric light, flush toilet, fan, air conditioner, vacuum cleaner and fax machine were all designed, developed and produced by men. They ride to work in transportation invented by men, on roads or rails built by men, to work in buildings designed and constructed by men. Every product that they use, right down to the most intimate products of feminine hygiene, were invented and produced by men. American women are more dependent upon men for what they have, than women have ever been since the beginning of civilization.

If the effect of the masculine Gender were removed from the economy, the American woman would be barefoot and in a grass skirt within one generation. This is not stated jokingly, or figuratively, but literally. In the winter of 1992 - 1993 there will be thousands of Eastern European women who will go barefoot and hungry. They will do this because they are living in an economy that has very little NEW.

It is NEW that feeds the burgeoning population of the world, it is NEW that cares for its health, it is NEW that clothes the masses, it is NEW that informs and educates. NEW is the result of the creative Will of the universe, the manifestation of masculine Gender. NEW is the natural product of the Capitalistic economy. NEW is what has brought the world this far. NEW is what the world needs more of in order to maintain its growth.

However, the societies of the world are working against the NEW. The only difference between the Soviet Union and the United States was a difference of degree. In the Soviet Union, the State and various bureaucracies determined what new products would be developed and produced. In America, the government, big business and big unions, meet to make decisions as to which industries need financing, protection, or special consideration. Yet, NEW does not come from the government, or the unions or big business. NEW comes from the conceptual thinking of individuals. It comes from the entrepreneur, or if he is not the inventor, from a joint effort on the part of the inventor and the entrepreneur. Does our government foster entrepreneurial activity? Not when it guarantees a one billion dollar loan to Chrysler Corporation, one billion dollars that individual business people would no longer have access to. Thousands of small businesses became stagnant or went bankrupt because they did not have sufficient funding at that time. It can be said that keeping Chrysler alive preserved many jobs but in fact no jobs were preserved; it only the location of the jobs. The same number of cars would have been built in America, with or without Chrysler. What was accomplished by that action was to protect a big business and a big union at the expense of small business and the nation. NEW does not come from big business or big unions. We should be thankful that at the time of buggy whip makers and kerosene lamp manufacturers, there were no big unions or big businesses involved in the manufacture of those products.

In the December 22, 1991 edition of the New York Times, the business section contained an interview with three economists concerning their opinions as to what President Bush should do about the economy. One of them, Lawrence A. Kudlow, chief economist at Bear Stearns & Company Inc. said, "If economic policy is operating against the innovator, against the risk-taker, we're going to see a very low rate of employment increase." The risk takers are not government, big business, or big unions. The risk takers are individuals who have the pioneering spirit, courage and creativity to bring NEW into the market place.

It is those people who are being constrained by the current credit crunch, and who have been constrained by governmental policies for decades, making it increasingly difficult for them to create NEW. A disproportionate share of the wealth of this nation has gone into real estate, not because of the need for housing, but because it became a vehicle of financial speculation supported by governmental policies. When real estate was not getting the money, big business was. When big business wasn't, then the money was going into gold, other commodities and financial instruments. In the early 1980's when the prime rate reached 20.5%, fledgling businesses could not afford to pay those rates, and consequently went bankrupt. Now that the prime rate is 6%, the banks prefer to loan their money to credit card users at 20%. Even during the 1970's, when the SBA had huge sums of money to dispense, the recipients of their largess had to be in hard core unemployed areas, or be minority-owned businesses, with the goal being job creation, rather than NEW creation.

This nation is choking off the creative urge of those men and women who possess the risk-taking, pioneering ability to bring NEW to the market place. Even venture capitalists are hardly venturing anymore, preferring to invest in businesses that are already started, that have management, customers, suppliers, payables and receivables. The entire financial community has lost its interest in supporting those who can create NEW. Instead it invests money in the old, the proven, the established, all of which are really the dying. IBM can get lots and lots of money, but IBM is on the same path traveled by Penn Central, Eastern Airlines and others that stopped creating NEW. Only NEW survives. Old businesses and corporations survive only if they continually create NEW. When NEW stops, the end begins. The end has begun for most large corporations and for the economic health of this nation. Government, big business and big unions can do little to stave off the inevitable consequences of stifled entrepreneurship. Only the unleashing of the creative Will of the populace will move the economy upward and onward, for it will create NEW, and NEW creates jobs for all people.

XXIV
Plato, Ayn Rand, Bachelors and Childless People

The Republic contains intellectual discourse in its highest form. It is pure objectivity, conceptual thinking, and abstract reasoning. It is also devoid of an understanding of the differences in Gender. It indicates that men and women can do the same things, and although men generally are superior in ability, both sexes should be given equal opportunities in all endeavors. *The Republic* contains masculine thinking within the confines of the feminine European psyche.

Some of the conclusions reached by Plato and his contemporaries were: children should be separated from their parents and turned over to the state; there shall be no requirements of fidelity between men and women; business and commerce are not admirable occupations; there are only two purposes for the study of mathematics - the evolvement of the philosophical mind and for military operations; there shall be no elections or choice of leadership; there shall be no need for lawyers; and the State shall be ruled by philosopher kings.

Many of Plato's recommendations have been implemented in varying degrees by our government, resulting in disastrous consequences. The State has taken over more and more of the function of raising children, infidelity has increased, and business is not held in high regard. As a result academic performance has decreased, crime has increased, family ties have weakened, entrepreneurship has faltered, and creativity has declined.

Plato's work exemplified masculine thinking within the limits of the European feminine psyche; his abstract reasoning was limited to material considerations. He had little understanding of the purpose and meaning of life. He also had the limited thinking of an unmarried person. People who love their children do not give them away except under duress. Men and women who have an appreciation and respect for each other do not readily share themselves with others. Plato's mentor Socrates was one of the few married men amongst his friends, and his wife Xanthippe, was considered to be a shrew. Socrates explained that it was an example of his practice of philosophy that enabled him to live with her. It would have been interesting to hear Xanthippe's version of the marriage.

Plato had no understanding of the creative will of the masculine Gender and did not realize that this creative will would lead to inventiveness that would supply products and services that would enable the population to expand rapidly and assist in the material and spiritual growth of humankind. And while he wrote extensive metaphysical treatises on the immortality of the soul, he nevertheless had no concept of spiritual evolvement. In fact, Plato had no concept of the general evolvement of humankind, its spiritual nature, and the differences of Gender. *The Republic*, unbeknownst to its author, is a scholarly treatise on grossly materialistic thinking.

Teachings emanating from an imbalance of Gender result in conclusions that are insensitive, tyrannical and iconoclastic, whether they were written by the ancient Plato or the modern Ayn Rand. Rand's male characters were ambitious, successful, tenacious, just, intelligent, and powerful. They were a woman's dream of the ideal man, and after reading her books, many a woman romanticized that she would find such a man. While Rand idolized powerful men and accomplished women, she had little regard for the mediocre, the untalented, the weak, and the relatively unintelligent. In her book *"Atlas Shrugged"*, she created an aristocracy of the competent, who eventually formed a society that excluded the rest of the people. Rand propounded the positive manifestations of the masculine gender but they were limited to the sphere of feminine materialistic thinking.

It is the nature of men to govern and to rule, but the purpose of their rulership is to provide the means and the environment for women to bring life into this world and nurture it. Childless people like Plato and Rand miss the point of human existence and purpose. Ruling and producing are not done for their own sake, but for the development of the race.

When ideologies are created that speak of "them and us", they are doomed to failure at the outset. There is only one ideology that serves the human race, and that is one that is concerned for all people. Since we are imperfect people, we create imperfect ideologies, but we must at least aim for the goal of consideration for all, and this can only be attained by a balanced Gender influence in society.

In the following chapter we will deal with the myth of "good" and "bad" people.

XXV
On Good and Bad People

There are only good people.

The classification of people as good and bad is a relative classification, essentially measuring the extent to which these people adhere to the standards of the person or group doing the judging.

Good and bad are on the same plane, much as, hot and cold, big and small, light and dark, quiet and noisy, are on the same planes. The differences between all these categories are relative. A room temperature of 85 degrees is considered to be hot, a cup of coffee at that temperature is considered to be cold. A big pile of topsoil is smaller than a small mountain. A brightly lit street is darker than a dark and dreary day. A noisy library is quieter than a quiet running truck engine. All physical measures are relative, and so are all measures concerning the actions of people.

Spiritually enlightened people in all parts of the world have established codes of conduct in order to assist humankind on its path of spiritual evolvement. One of these standards is the Ten Commandments. The first three of these commandments have to do with our relationship to God, but with the realization that we can not have a relationship to God if we are not here, the other seven commandments have to do with our relationship to each other. We cannot long survive if we steal from each other, kill one another, commit adultery, be disrespectful, or do any of the other acts that the commandments warn us against. To the degree that we comply with these commandments we are called "good", to the degree that we do not comply, we are called "bad". Since no one can comply with all the commandments completely, no one can be completely "good", and since everyone complies to some degree, no one can be completely "bad". We enact laws that generally are at a level commensurate with the average performance of society. Those people that can comply are considered to be good, and those that can't are considered to be bad. If the laws are such that only a few people can comply, the laws are considered to be too stringent. If the laws are such that almost anybody can comply, then they are considered to be to lax. These codes of conduct are necessary for the functioning of societal order, and to the degree that they are within range of what the average of people can reasonably comply with, they are considered to be just.

The differences between "good" and "bad" people are differences in evolvement or understanding, similar to the difference in knowledge between someone who has only studied basic arithmetic and someone who has studied calculus. One is "good" in mathematics and one is "bad" in mathematics. The difference between the two people is one of knowledge and understanding. And so is the moral difference between people. We should not lower the moral goal anymore than we should lower the scholastic goal. And as we should equally love the high performer in mathematics and the low performer, we must also love the highly moral and the immoral. Even when reprimanding the immoral, punishing them, or even executing them in accordance with our laws, we must remember that in the absolute sense, they are all "good".

This concept of "goodness" applies to nations as well. There are no "good" and "bad" nations, or "good" and "bad" leaders. All leaders are representative of the average will of the people, and they come into power because of the expectation of the people that these leaders will bring about the conditions that they (the people) want. The particular types of government that these leaders create are merely vehicles to overthrow the existing order, so that change can be brought about. The form of government that was most prevalent from the mid 19th to the mid 20th century was the aristocracy. There were aristocracies of: family name, religion, race, wealth, property ownership, and ethnicity. The aristocracies were toppled and new governments, both on the left and on the right, established. Now those governments are toppling, and are again being replaced by new and different forms of government.

"Bad governments and good" governments are determined by the victors, for the history books are written by the victors. The Mexicans were "bad" and the United States was "good", the South was "bad" and the North was "good", the Axis powers were "bad" and the Allies were "good", the USSR was "bad" and NATO was "good". In the present tense "bad" are those who do not think as we do, and "good" are those who think as we do. Communism is "bad" and democracy is "good". Iran, Iraq, Syria, Egypt and Israel, have been both "good" and "bad", according to what has served the best interests of the United States. Victors write the history books, make history. The only thing to be learned from history is that nothing is to be learned from history, because history is a record made by the victors and taught by the victors. There are no "good" and "bad" governments, they are all vehicles used by the people to bring about change at a desired time.

There is but one God, one creation, and one people. That God, and that universe, and the people in it are good. It cannot be otherwise. We have all come from the one source, and we are all on an infinite journey to return to it. We are all brothers and sisters in the most literal sense, and we are all good, regardless of our differences. Actually, differences have to do with our viewpoint, and while we all have viewpoints, none of us have the full view. Therefore we criticize each other for not seeing what we see.

I write this chapter on "good" and "bad" people because of the rapidly developing attitude in our country, and the world for that matter, of "them" and "us". As I have indicated in my article on tolerance, I believe this nation is a very tolerant and cooperative nation, yet almost every difference of opinion we read or hear about, has to do with "them" or "us". We have right versus left, pro abortion versus anti abortion, believers versus atheists, black versus whites, environmentalists versus industrialists, poor versus rich, old versus young, married versus single, on and on we go, drawing lines around us and others, creating enmity amongst our brothers and sisters. Differences of opinion are wonderful, and we all learn from opposing viewpoints, but when we begin to see those who think differently form us as "bad", then we are creating disharmony in the family.

We behave as we do because we have lost a sense of individual and national purpose. We have no leadership at present, because, we wanted none. We liked the narcissistic life, the "do one's own thing," the freedom, the lack of restraint no longer imposed by the manifestation of the masculine Gender. Now we are living in the chaos that results from lack of order, and we are blaming everyone but ourselves. As the great American philosopher Pogo has said, "We have met the enemy, and they are us", is a truism, and we should look in the mirror for the cause of or present situation, and not blame our brothers and sisters.

Keep the faith my brothers and sisters, love each other, and know that each person whom you see, no matter how different in any respect, is a part of your family, and is GOOD.

XXVI
Wives and Mothers

The loyal wife and devoted mother has done more to keep society functioning than has any other person or institution.

She has bathed her family in love, nurtured and motivated them, and by example, has imparted to them the positive human values. She has made her husband a hero to their children and a success unto himself. There was no hardship that she would not endure for the benefit of her family, no matter too small for her attention, and no task too troublesome. She has fueled the race with the power of her love, propelling it to all manner of accomplishment.

She involved herself in the education of her children by being active with the school system. She gave of her time to the Boy Scouts, Girl Scouts, or community youth activities. She was active in the practice of her faith and gave her children a religious orientation. She was awake all hours of the night bringing down fevers and attending to the sickness of the family. She furnished a home with the material items that would add to the comfort and well being of all. She was involved in car pools or other joint activities that enabled her children to engage in athletic, dance, music or scholarly activities. She created a social life for her husband, an environment for him to relax in, and catered to his every need. Her conduct was a reflection on him, and she did him honor. This woman was not only an asset to the family, tribe and race, she was their very essence.

She has earned her stripes, and is deserving of the highest honors and accolades; yet, she receives no recognition. When asked by strangers what she does, and she responds that she is a wife and mother, they will usually then ask, "What else do you do?" Nurturing the race, caring for the young, giving, and loving, are not considered to be doing anything in today's chaotic and narcissistic society. Even other women, when in various volunteer organizations, will delegate more work to her because "she stays at home and doesn't do anything". To be a wife and mother does not seem by many to be worthy of commendation, however, to be a mother and not a wife, that gets plenty of recognition and reward.

Unwed mothers account for 25% of the newborn, and are rewarded by the State with multitudinous financial aid, health benefits, and vocational training. Their children are raised without the benefit of a masculine influence in the home, and therefore are not exposed to the traits necessary to assume the responsibilities of adulthood, and more specifically manhood. This is preparing another generation for unwed motherhood, and an increasing control of the societal function by the State.

It is a tragedy that the loyal wife and devoted mother, who not only does not require support from the State, but because of her supportive roll enables a man to contribute to the financial well-being of society, should be held in less esteem than the unwed mother, who deprives her child of a natural familial environment, is committed to no man, and who is an economic drain on society.

How much longer is this distortion of natural conduct and its resultant damage to society, to continue, before men act?

XXVII
Tolerance in America

After disposing of my manufacturing business, I started a consulting business and my first client was a white, Jewish, South African fashion designer. His employees were a male Iranian Muslim cutter, and a female black American Christian sample maker. The three of them worked diligently to make the fledgling company a success. Would these same people have been able to associate as freely in South Africa, Iran or Israel?

We have had a black representative to the United Nations, on the Supreme Court, Chairman of the Joint Chiefs of Staff, and a presidential candidate. Is there any white nation in this world that had similar representation? Is there any black nation that had whites in similar positions?

Our representatives to the Olympiads come from all ethnic, racial and religious backgrounds, their distinguishing characteristic being that they are indistinguishable from the representatives of other nations. Our domestic professional sports also contain people from every ethnic, racial and religious affiliation.

In the area of volunteerism, an activity that keeps this nation functioning, there is a pulling together, a sharing and sacrificing between a diversity of peoples that is unparalleled by any other nation.

Our judicial system provides a trial by a jury consisting of our peers, and what a wonderful experience it is to be a part of that jury. If there is any doubt that a diverse group of people can lay aside all differences and do their utmost to be fair to an individual, that doubt will be dispelled by one term on jury duty. I had the good fortune to be on jury duty for a civil case in which the membership of the jury contained black, white and oriental; low, middle and high income; and an age mixture in the 20's, 30's, 40's, 50's and 60's. We worked as one entity to be as fair as we were able, in judging the case. I feel secure in the knowledge that should I ever be a defendant in a trial judged by my peers, I will be getting the fairest consideration humanly possibly, regardless of the ethnic, religious or racial makeup of the jury.

For eight years I had my manufacturing company located in East Orange, New Jersey, a city that has the second highest percentage black population in America. There was never any animosity shown towards me as a white business owner, and quite to the contrary, one day when I was in the parking lot getting into my Mercedes a group of young black men passing by gave me a thumbs up in recognition of what they perceived as my success. Prior to East Orange, my business was located in a predominantly Hispanic section of Newark, New Jersey. Again there was no evidence of prejudice towards me, and in time, a very friendly relationship was developed between a significant portion of the community and me.

In 1989 New York Magazine published an article concerning prejudice, which I challenged, and my comments were printed in the letters to the editor section. Shortly thereafter, I had dinner at a sidewalk restaurant on Manhattan's Upper West Side. My date was a Japanese woman, at the table to my left were a black man and a white woman, two tables to my right were a white man and a black woman, and walking by us were an oriental man and a black Hispanic woman. This was hardly a setting indicative of a supposedly prejudicial society.

For prejudicial societies it is necessary to look outside of the United States. With the collapse of the USSR there arose ethnic tensions throughout Eastern Europe and ethnic warfare in some countries. In Africa there is tribal warfare to this day. The American Indians had tribal conflicts up until the time that the government of the United States was imposed upon them. There is ethnic and religious tension and conflict in India, Sri Lanka, Pakistan, Israel, Iran, Cyprus, Northern Ireland, and Spain.

If there is any nation in this world that exemplifies the ability of a diversity of people to work together, it is the United States. People from all over the world have been literally dying in their attempts to be admitted to our country. It is known throughout the world that America is the land of opportunity to all peoples. At the time that I was a high school student, the three major immigrant groups were Germans, Italians and Jews. I attended Brooklyn Technical High School, a school that specialized in engineering and had an enrollment of 6,400 students, the majority of whom had foreign born parents. The exemplary work of the students posted in the hallways had names on them such as Schmidt, Conte and Epstein, which was indicative of the major immigrant groups of the period, and how their children were motivated to excel. When visiting Brooklyn Tech 40 years later, the names on the work posted in the hallways were Kim, Patel, and Ogino, which were indicative of the Korean, Indian and Japanese immigrants that were then prevalent in our nation, and whose offspring were making their impact on our society. People of diverse backgrounds have been continually making positive contributions to our culture and economy, and it cannot be otherwise. We are a nation of diversity that functions very, very well.

Areas of apparent intolerance stem from two causes; the first being a natural loyalty to the tribe, which was very strong during the early part of this century, as was explained in the chapter Tyranny at Home. The tribal orientations were ethnic, religious and racial, and frequently combinations of the three groupings. Ethnicity was a result of people living within geographical boundaries. As transportation and communications increased in a capitalistic society, the movement of different ethnic groups increased, to the point that ethnicity in America is rapidly disappearing. Religious groupings were based essentially on differing perceptions of the one God. As our perceptions broaden, the apparent religious differences decrease. Racial groupings are a result of broad geographical origins, but the resultant differences in color are temporary manifestations in the evolvement of the human race. The day is approaching when first in America, and then throughout the world, we shall be one race worshiping one God, each according to our own perceptions.

The second cause for apparent intolerance stems from economic and societal concerns. It is a natural trait to emulate the powerful and avoid the weak. "Success has many suitors, but failure is truly an orphan" is a phrase introduced to me by a customer many years ago, the veracity of which is proven to me on a frequent basis. While it is also natural to want to help the weak, it is not natural to be as them. Therefore when our economy, safety, and educational standards are threatened, there is a tendency to be at first defensive of our position, and then aggressive to those that are making the incursion. Every tribal grouping in America has at one time been on the low end of the social and economic ladder and has incurred the hostile attitude of those outside of the tribe. However, every tribal grouping has also worked itself out of poverty and has been leveled up and assimilated into the mainstream of American culture as a result of the capitalistic economy and the spirit of free enterprise that exists in this nation.

This ability to work oneself out of poverty has been severely impeded by the increasingly socialistic bent of our domestic policy, which rewards failure, taxes success, emasculates the males, fosters unwed motherhood, destroys the family, and credentializes people out of the job market. When people are unable to level themselves up, and require the forced assistance of others for their livelihood, the others begin to rebel. Those that do the rebelling are accused of being prejudiced by those who have created the condition of enforced poverty. This same condition now exists in Eastern Europe after a century of unsuccessful living under socialism. These conditions are not racially motivated; they are politically created.

The removal of the negative socialist-inspired laws and the promulgation of family values, free enterprise, spiritual values and the resultant morality, will enable people to level themselves up, thus eliminating the hostility of those who were forced to support them in their poverty.

Intolerance in America is less than in any other society of diverse cultures. It is a politically created condition, which causes us to behave contrary to the natural American behavior. We are all brothers and sisters, and we have shown that we can work, play, study, live together, and defend each other on a consistent basis.

Keep the faith my brothers and sisters, do not follow false prophets, love one another, and work to bring about the conditions that will be most conducive to the attainment of our earthly and spiritual purposes.

XXVIII
The Inhibitors
of Success

There will be many who will disagree with the position taken in the last chapter, and who will insist that there is a great deal of prejudice in America. There are newspapers that rely upon the propagation and acceptance of that viewpoint in order to sustain their readership. There are non-profit organizations that owe their existence to the belief in the existence of prejudice. There are government agencies whose sole function is to combat this perceived prejudice. These people, organizations, and government agencies spend considerable sums of taxpayer money on the propagation of information that supports the belief that rampant prejudice exists and inhibits the success and well being of those who are the victims of this perceived prejudice. The victimizers are-as we shall see-those who spread the doctrine of victimization.

In order for people to create, build, accomplish, and prosper, they must have the belief that they can do it. Disbelief in one's ability cannot result in positive accomplishment. To continually hear negative statements and comments about oneself or one's societal grouping has the effect of a negative affirmation. Children who hear negative affirmations such as: you'll never amount to anything, you'll never marry a decent man, you'll never make much money, you're a bad boy, you're an ugly girl, no decent person would go out with you, no decent woman would become your wife; are children who have had failure drummed into them and whose likelihood of success and happiness are remote.

When these children become adults they are again exposed to negative comments such as: you'll never be treated fairly, you're getting a third rate education, they don't give women an even chance, they don't like Hispanics, old people are rarely hired, those companies don't hire blacks. The list of negative assertions is truly unlimited. If the negativity of childhood wasn't enough to hold them back, a whole new set of negative affirmations is thrust upon them many times each day as adults, again reinforcing the concept of failure.

The media, press, various organizations, and government continue this negative deluge with statements such as: the "filthy" rich, the successful people who "live only for themselves", "those" people in power, and businessmen can't be "trusted". What these statements are doing is telling the people they shouldn't be rich, successful, powerful or in business.

If a young man somehow survived the negativity that enveloped his youth, if he pushed through the negativity of early adulthood thrust upon him by the media and various organizations, if he developed a set of positive values that wealth, success, power and business achievement were worthy objectives, he still had to face another hurdle of negativity. He would be exposed to the following: men abuse women, men are no good, men don't make good parents, men are lazy, men subjugate women, and on and on and on.

From childhood to adulthood, through adulthood into old age, there is a constant barrage of negativity thrown upon people, the effects of which are debilitating, especially to males, for nothing happens in this universe until it is initiated by the masculine Gender, and if the masculine Gender is repressed and not motivated, what then can it initiate?

More negativity is thrown upon the people but in the guise of beneficence. "You were destined to suffer in this earthly life, but you will get your reward in heaven." How comforting. You have gone through childhood, adulthood and old age only to learn that this was a practice run—that the prize has to be obtained later and elsewhere.

Is it any wonder that upward mobility is becoming more difficult? A caste system has been created in America, not by those who have achieved, who are wealthy, accomplished and successful, but by those who have not achieved, and who are not wealthy, accomplished or successful. They earn their livelihood off the backs of the people who they claim they are helping, but who they are really enslaving by a constant barrage of put-downs. These people are the victimizers of society, preaching negativity and dissension to the masses, and profiting there from.

There is a positive philosophy that can be preached to the people. It gives people the confidence to strive, to reach, to imagine. It is a philosophy that incorporates the fundamental law of cause and effect which is most often stated as "whatsoever a man soweth, that shall he also reap." It is a philosophy that believes "ask and it shall be given", "seek and you shall find." The statement "whatsoever you ask for in prayer, believe that you have received it, and it shall be yours" is intrinsic to this philosophy. It is a philosophy that believes in each human being there is a WILL that can bring about any change the individual wants. It is a philosophy that teaches that every person has access to all the knowledge that exists—"the Holy Spirit is within you, you need no other teachers." It is a philosophy that motivates people to be in charge of their own destinies.

Why hasn't this positive philosophy prevailed? Why do we make excuses for our failure to succeed? Why are we so receptive to the negative philosophy? The answer to these questions and a multitude of others that can be asked along the same vein is that we are living in a feminine Gender oriented society. Only the will of the masculine gender can implement a positive philosophy.

In every relationship or marriage there will be those situations in which the woman says "you don't appreciate me," "you don't like me anymore," "you don't love me anymore," "you don't recognize all that I do," "you treat me like I'm part of the furniture," "you abuse me," "you don't think I'm pretty," "you yell at me," etc. etc. etc. In a Gender balanced marital and relationship situation these feelings are resolved, or at least coped with, and life goes on in a reasonably positive direction. However, in a society that has a weak masculine influence, these feelings are not resolved or coped with, and life does not continue in a positive direction but becomes passive, feminine receptive. The perception expands that ALL are abused, whether it be because of age, color, sex, religion, ethnicity, education, or a host of other reasons. A resurgence of the influence of the masculine Gender must become manifest in order to reverse this trend.

The masculine Gender takes responsibility for its condition and situation, and takes the appropriate ACTION to remedy the conditions and situations that it considers to be adverse. The masculine Gender is responsive to the needs, desires, frustrations, and fears of the feminine Gender and does what is necessary to fulfill, alleviate or remedy these emotional expressions. Once the masculine Gender reasserts itself in society the inhibitors of change will pass from influence.

XXIX
Our Brothers
in Prison

We have the highest rate of incarceration in the world, which is another way of saying that no other societal grouping throws more of its own into jail.

The following is an excerpt from a paragraph under the subject Prison, in the 1971 edition of the Encyclopedia Britannica: "In the United States, where crime rates have been among the highest observed in modern societies, there are well over 200,000 prisoners confined in more than 200 state and federal prisons and reformatories, with an annual increase in the prisoner population of approximately 4,500. Current trends indicate that the number of prisoners will continue to increase."

At the rate of increase of 4,500 per year, the prison population would have reached 290,000 by 1991. The prison population in 1991 reached 1,000,000; a figure limited by the number of cells available. Meanwhile, new laws are being proposed that will increase the number of incarcerations.

Why are 1,000,000 of our brothers in jail, and more waiting to get in? Why is this nation, which represents freedom to people throughout the world, putting more and more of its citizens in jail?

The current incarceration rate in the United States is 426 for every 100,000 of population. In South Africa it is 333 per 100,000, and in the Soviet Union it is 268 per 100,000. Of these two other nations, one is going through a major political change, and the other is experiencing economic collapse and political disintegration. Why does our incarceration rate exceed that of these nations?

Why is it that during the latter part of the 20th century, a period of a pronounced influence of feminine Gender, which manifested itself in all forms of nurturing such as: concern for wildlife whether it be caribou in Alaska, spotted owls in the northwest, dolphins in the Pacific, elephants in Africa, or rabbits in pharmaceutical labs; the environment whether it be the rain forests in Brazil or the erosion of our beaches; the quality of environment whether it be for cleaner air or water; there is little concern for the men in prison? Is not an American man worthy of the same attention and consideration as the caribou, tuna and spotted owl?

In the early part of this century there were very few men in prison, not only in absolute numbers, but also as a percentage of the population. By 1960 the prison population increased several-fold, the increase outpacing the increase in population. However, it was after the 1960's that the prison population surged, increasing six-fold in 25 years.

The amount of social legislation was minimal in the beginning of the century, increased significantly by mid-century and then expanded tremendously as a result of the Great Society legislation of the 1960's.

This parallel between the growth of prison population and social legislation should not be underestimated, for as the influence of government increases in society, the influence of free men decreases and more of them are imprisoned. This was the case in the Soviet Union. Also, as the influence of free men decreases, the influence of the government will increase. As men fulfill their responsibilities, the influence of government will decrease, as men shirk their responsibilities, the influence of government will increase.

Reasons for the increase of the prison population have been attributed to poverty, race, education and ethnicity. These are not causative factors. They are resultant factors. As government growth increasingly emasculates males, giving them less control over their lives, their families, and the tribe, males have less and less opportunity to extricate themselves from adverse economic and social conditions.

Great Society legislation had a ruinous effect on the familial and tribal structure. This legislation rewarded mothers for not having husbands, passed laws prohibiting natural Gender differences between the sexes, removed the moral standards of society from the tribe and put it in the hands of the government, stifled entrepreneurial activity, and created a welfare mentality. Great Society legislation is responsible for: the one million of our brothers who are living in cages, the one million of our youth who are gang members and who are shooting each other dead in the streets, the 100,000 of our sisters who are raped annually, the decline of academic performance, the decline of moral standards, the stagnation of our economy, the narcissistic philosophy, and the societal chaos that is everywhere.

Great Society legislation has inhibited men from fulfilling their natural masculine Gender roles in the family and tribe. Consequently the government assumed more of the role in the care of women and children. It provided housing, money, food stamps, medical attention, education, and counseling; all activities normally attended to by men. These activities by the government became self-perpetuating at an increasing rate. Young males were raised in an environment without the influence of a male role model, without an understanding of the responsibilities of manhood, therefore they grew up unprepared and unmotivated to assume the role of head of the family.

This cycle of emasculation is being exacerbated by the general ignorance of society regarding the importance of Gender. On December 4, 1991 CBS News at 12 noon reported that 25% of all American children are born to single mothers, that two thirds of teenage pregnancies occur to single girls, and that 90% of black children are born to single mothers. Immediately following the announcement of these horrific figures, guest Ann Pleshette

Murphy, Editor in Chief of Parents Magazine, commented that television programming for children was sexist because it portrayed men as heros. Well, not to worry Ann, with that thinking, more and more of our mothers will be unwed, more males will be raised without knowing the responsibilities of manhood, and indeed, there will be fewer heroes.

Gender is the issue. In the broader context, most of our brothers who are incarcerated are political prisoners. They are the result of a government that has passed laws depriving them of the exercise of their manhood, inhibiting their natural inclination to be the head of the family and part of the rulership of the tribe. They are the result of broken homes, homelessness, social and educational neglect. They have not been advised, guided, motivated, counseled or loved. As a punishment for not adjusting to the environment thrust upon them, they are sent to jail (those who were fortunate to have survived the slaughter in the streets) where they get even less motivation and love.

Our penal system is an anachronism that is inhumane and ineffective. It neither deters people from criminal action, nor rehabilitates those that have committed crimes. However, it is not the purpose of this book to elaborate on an overhaul of the penal system, but to point out that we have within the system political prisoners in the truest meaning of that term. The manhood of this nation should not be wasted in prison, and we should do our utmost to see that the level of incarceration of our brothers decreases.

So long as society focuses on race, ethnicity, poverty, education, or any other issue, the primary cause of our expanding prison population will not be addressed. The primary issue is one of Gender. Ethnicity is passing rapidly, religious differences are narrowing, differences in color are fading, but the difference in Gender will always be. Only when men and women realize their responsibilities to one another, to the family, tribe and race (the human race), and contribute their respective unique talents to the propagation and preservation of the race, will we have a relatively harmonious and healthy society, that incarcerates a minimal number of its members.

XXX
Gravitations to and from the Gender Balance

"Do something" is the statement made to men by women round-the-world, when there is a problem to be solved or trouble to be coped with.

We laugh and joke about this, and feminists burn their bras over it, but it is the natural reaction of individuals and groups, when in trouble, to immediately seek out the more masculine influence for assistance. It is this natural inclination, and the expectation of this more masculine influence to perform, that is an integral part of the preservation of the species.

During periods of armed conflict, nations seek the leadership of the strongest most masculine manifestation available. In World War I the French recalled from retirement Clemenceau, "the Tiger of France", to deal with the advance of the German armies, and later to inflict the punishment of the Treaty of Versailles. He was the biggest meanest manifestation of masculinity that could be found for the job. In World War II Churchill, was called upon to rally the nation in its battle against the Axis powers. He was known among his own people as "the British Hitler", and preferred to hang the German leadership rather than have the Nuremburg trials proposed by Stalin. "Emergency powers" were granted to Lincoln at the beginning of the Civil War, and to Roosevelt at the beginning of World War II. Gorbachev requested "emergency powers" when the Soviet Union began to crumble, and Yeltsen is currently operating with the authority of "emergency powers." All "emergency powers" means, is the right to the unbridled manifestation of the masculine Gender, and preferably in its extreme form, brutality. However, people instinctively know that to have this extreme of masculine Gender in the position of leadership when an emergency does not exist, can lead to tyrannical governments, and the people therefore, remove this type of leadership as soon as the crisis is over.

Clemenceau left office after the Treaty of Versailles, and Churchill was voted out of office in the first election after World War II. Emergency powers were removed in Washington after the Civil War and World War II. Even though rulership is a masculine function, there is an inherent distrust by the population when it senses an imbalance of Gender in the government. The American electorate in 1976 decided that after having two powerful presidents, it was time for a less powerful chief executive, and it voted accordingly. The feeling of that presidency was illustrated by an event that occurred during a presidential visit to New York City. I was in my car on Sixth Avenue when traffic was stopped because of the presidential motorcade crossing ahead. There was a truck on each side of me, and one trucker said to the other "what's going on?" The other trucker said, "Jimmy's in town." The first trucker said, "Jimmy who?" After four years of "Jimmy who," the voters decided it was time again for an assertive leadership. Likewise, in 1952 after a long period of assertive presidents, the voters elected General Eisenhower, who for eight years ran a highly unassertive administration, the joke at the time being, "have you seen the Eisenhower doll, you wind it up and it does nothing for eight years?" After eight years of nothingness, the electorate decided it was time for a more masculine manifestation of Gender in government, and served up two strong presidential candidates.

This same gravitation towards the masculine Gender in times of difficulty occurs in business as well. As mentioned earlier, Chrysler went to the government when it was in economic trouble, Eastern Europe has come to us in time of economic trouble, and our government went to Japan when it was in economic trouble; the latter being a very sad spectacle, and an indication to the world of the lack of masculinity on the American domestic scene. Any individual, group, organization, business or nation, when in trouble, will always look to the more masculine manifestation of Gender for help.

This desire for assistance from the masculine Gender is a natural reaction, as is the desire to have it go away when the crises is over. Every woman wants a strong man around the house, someone whom she can rely on in times of need or moments of stress. However, she does not want that strong influence around her constantly. She wants to be able to operate freely in her arena with a minimum interference on the part of the man. However, if there is trouble, if she was treated disrespectfully by her boss, or the mechanic, or the bank, then she likes to be able to go and get her big gorilla, or her lion from the cage, trot him down to the mechanic and let him growl a few times, bring him home, put him back in the cage, and then go about her business.

The negative effects of the excess of masculine Gender are obvious to most people, and as has been shown, we tend to instinctively guard against these excesses. What however, is not as readily recognized is the excesses that occur when there is an imbalance of Gender in the feminine direction, or more properly put, when there is an insufficient manifestation of the masculine Gender. This holds true in our domestic life as well. We read and hear about rapes, beatings, muggings and murders. On the other hand, we do not read or hear about the lack of masculinity in the home, where its effects are only recognized long after the fact. Masculinity operates in an overt manner, whereas femininity operates in a covert manner.

In the following chapter we shall see the insidious effects of the inadequate manifestation of the masculine Gender.

XXXI
Effects of Gravitations Away from the Masculine Gender

One of the products that my firm manufactured was a tarpaulin, a covering used as an enclosure on high rise buildings to hold in the heat when concrete is poured, allowing it time to cure. On one shipment of tarpaulins we had placed the grommets in the wrong location, and it was decided to send a crew to the jobsite to make appropriate corrections. One employee selected to be part of the crew was a 19 year old youth. When he was asked to go to New York (we were located in Newark, NJ) he refused. I explained that he would be driven to the jobsite by my partner, and would be working with three other men. He still refused. I decided to nettle him and said to him, "Are you a man or a boy," and he replied, "I'm a boy, ask my mother." Flabbergasted, I sent him back into the shop. A few moments later Bea, my floor lady came into my office and said to me, "I guess you know that we have a boy working for us." I asked, "Did he tell you too", and she said, "He told everybody." The next morning his mother called to make sure that I understood that her son was just a boy.

That event did not make the newspapers or the evening television news the way that an act of extreme masculine Gender would have. There isn't anything newsworthy about a good-looking nineteen year old earning a living and residing with his parents. Nevertheless, the effect on this man's life would be devastating. Would a woman want to be married to him? Could he make any family decisions? Could he be a role model to his children? Would he be a man that a woman would want to lean on? Would he be a protector of society? While this extreme lack of masculine Gender was not immediately newsworthy, the effects would eventually become newsworthy when the breakdown of the societal structure resulting from this lack of manliness became evident.

Author Deborah Tannen explains that men and women communicate differently in her book *"You Just Don't Understand,"* one of many books, articles, and programs inundating us lately concerning the differences between the sexes. The Wall Street Journal had an article indicating that infant mortality is lower when there are fathers in the home, and other articles published elsewhere indicated that SAT scores are higher when there are fathers in the home. At this rate of evolvement we might know by the end of this decade, what the cave man knew. Getting back to Deborah Tannen, she mentions that men communicate to obtain information, and that women communicate to relate. This difference partially accounts for what is known as gossip among women, for it is not so much the subject matter that is important, as is the opportunity to relate. However, now that women are employed at all levels in the various media, communications are changing from being informative to being a vehicle for relating or entertaining. On all the morning news programs we have both men and women newscasters, and an ever-increasing non-informative banter that is extremely disconcerting to most men. What do I care whose TV mistress Connie Chung is or if Harry Smith had time to bathe? I want the news, that's all. But even when we get to the news, the accuracy level is low.

CBS THIS MORNING covered the retirement of Mike Schmidt, stating that he was one of the leading homerun hitters, but never mentioned how many homeruns he hit. A segment of a film clip taken two years earlier when he hit his 500th homerun was shown, and it was up to the viewer to extrapolate what the results were two years later. In another story, which paid homage to Frank Capra, they indicated that he had his favorite picture, but didn't say which one. If the viewer were old enough he might have recognized it as "Mr. Smith Goes To Washington." When a major derailment of the New York subway system occurred early in the fall of 1991, CBS THIS MORNING advised their viewers to take alternate means of transportation, but never mentioned which line or which station had the derailment. But then what does it matter, we might not know exactly what is happening, but we're relating.

The New York Times Sports Section, which had spent considerable money on TV advertising extolling the accuracy of its reporting, published an article on boxing showing Gene Tunney as heavyweight champion from 1878-1905. Actually Tunney took the crown from Jack Dempsey in the 1920's. The same article showed Max Schmeling's career lasting from 1924-1948, a 24-year boxing career! Well it was almost true; Schmeling served as a paratrooper in the weremacht from 1940 till the end of the war, and then did some boxing until 1948. When Nolan Ryan pitched his seventh no hitter, the article by the Times stated, "Summing up a game in which two-thirds of his 122 pitches were strikes;" a highly improbably set of figures for a no hit game especially since he faced only 29 batters. But then who's counting and what difference does it all make? We're all relating; isn't that nice nice.

So the networks don't provide accurate news coverage, so the Times has Gene Tunney fighting in the wrong century, so magazine articles ascribe quotes to the wrong person, or list statistics that do not apply to the subject matter. What's to worry? These are but mild covert excesses of the lack of masculinity and do not compare with the violence of the excesses of masculinity. Really? The SAT scores have dropped 25% and Johnny can't read, count, or speak very well either. I mentioned jokingly to a friend recently, that at the rate at which our verbal skills are declining, we'll soon be back to sign language. In January 1992 on network news, it was announced that two colleges were giving credit for sign language as a second language. No need to worry about spelling and punctuation marks with that course, and a high SAT performance is not a prerequisite.

The day that I completed this chapter, February 12, 1992, The Wall Street Journal ran an article entitled "Leaders of U.S. History Textbooks Discover a Storehouse of Misinformation," in which it was shown that there was a flagrant disregard for facts in the very texts that were being used to educate the nation. Such misinformation as: President Truman ending the war in Korea by dropping the "bomb" (the "bomb" was not dropped in Korea, and Eisenhower was President when the war ended), American troops met tremendous resistance in the Bay of Pigs invasion (American troops were not used in that invasion), the battle of Vicksburg was shown to have taken place in Tennessee (it took place in Mississippi—that's where Vicksburg is located).

Why go through the hypocrisy of telling our youth how the importance of an education, when the accuracy of the facts and figures of our media are questionable? Why point out the monetary success of an education to our youth, when they can see it is entertainment that gets the money, whether sports, recordings, films, or TV? Why tell our children to succeed in business when the only time they hear of business people in the media is when they are doing something wrong, whereas when entertainment people do the same thing the media refers to them as stars? Children do as they see and not as they are told, and our youth see that standards are not held in high regard by any person or institution, even those espousing standards. Compare this to a scene from the original Perry Mason series staring Raymond Burr, in which Perry counsels a youth and explains that a man's word is his bond; that men are to be trusted in what they say. Compare this to the phrase that has been heard on almost every comedy show of the past few years, "so I lied." Oh, and all the laughter that that phrase gets. So I lied! The current moral standards are no standards at all. Today, when a man shakes the hand of another, all that is known for sure is that they each have a hand.

This lack of masculinity and the consequent lack of standards has had a severe negative effect upon society, with women and children being the most victimized. It is natural for women to expect that a man's word is his bond, and is the foundation of the phrase that women use to call men to account when they say "you said." Every man has had women say to him "you said," the implication being that if he said it, he should be held accountable for what he said. Few women want to be married to a wimp, a weak kneed milksop, a peanut butter cookie (that confection, regardless of its external color, when cracked open, has yellow oozing out of it). Women expect that in times of trouble men will "do something." We now see on TV and in the print media women saying that rape will be controlled when "men do something about it." Yes, and SAT's will go up when "men do something about it," and teenage pregnancies will decrease when "men do something about it," and crime in the streets will decrease when "men do something about it." When men begin to realize why they are here, that they have an obligation to take care of the family, tribe and race, then there will be a reestablishment of standards in society, and they will "do something."

In the following chapter we will see how our natural masculine and feminine desires and manifestations are represented in our government.

XXXII
American Political Parties and Gender Identification

The current vehicle for the expression of the feminine Gender in American politics is the Democratic Party. The nurturing aspect of life is attributable to the feminine Gender, and is the reason the earth is referred to as Mother Earth, for she nurtures us all, regardless of whether we are deserving or not, whether we are old or young, rich or poor, ambitious or lazy, the earth's bounty is made available to all on an indiscriminate basis. Any female animal gives equal succor to all of her offspring regardless of their individual temperaments. Every human mother nurtures her children equally. It is this instinctive nurturing ability that causes men to want to be in the aura of a woman, and that creates a longing for her presence when they are removed from it for extended periods. The world needs to be nurtured, and nurturing comes from the feminine Gender aspect of our beings. In the political sense we see this nurturing aspect best expressed in the Democratic Party.

The Democratic Party caters to all people: young and old, the infirm, social outcasts, political radicals, rich and poor, all races, religions and ethnic groups. The Democratic Party offers unearned mother love, and the nurturing aspect of the feminine Gender. It attempts to provide these people with succor through various means such as aid to education, anti-discrimination laws, welfare, social security, minority set asides for municipal contacts, aid to dependent children, tax exemptions for the needy, government housing, and youth employment programs, which are some of the more popular of what seems to be an infinite assortment of programs to nurture the nation.

An extension of nurturing is coddling, and while the feminine nature is to coddle those whom she nurtures, the effects upon those who were excessively coddled can be debilitating, as was the case with the youth described in the last chapter. The manifestation of coddling in government is the proliferation of special interest groups, the debilitating effects of welfare, the bestowing of "rights" to individuals, such as rights to housing, rights to an education, rights to a job, and rights to happiness. Excessive coddling makes for spoiled dependent children, and in society it makes for spoiled dependent people. Coddled children become slaves of their mothers, and coddled people become slaves of the State.

The nature of nurturing is to give succor until there are none left to succor or until there is no milk left to give. In the Democratic Party this desire to give unlimited succor translates into the philosophy of spend, spend, spend. It appears that as a party, the Democrats have no concept of where money comes from. So ingrained is the philosophy of spending, that even in its excesses it is not noticed. In the 1988 elections, the Democratic standard bearer was governor of the state that had the severest economic problems. In 1992 the state with the second worst economic problems was New York, and there were those in the Democratic Party who wanted to draft the governor of New York for the Presidency. In the spring of 1979 I met at the bar of the Hotel Pierre in New York a European representative of the International Monetary Fund. He was a distinguished and very proper gentleman, and he whispered to me that he didn't mean to be derogatory about my President, but that Mr. Carter did not seem to have an understanding of economics. I replied that he didn't have to be reluctant to express his viewpoint, that he could stand up on the bar and shout it, for every American knew that. Mr. Carter was another Democratic governor who left his state in economic shambles.

Throughout this book, and probably to the consternation of many, I have indicated that creativity and the pioneering spirit are manifestations of the masculine Gender. Therefore, in a party that is essentially feminine Gender oriented, these qualities would be missing. In their book *"The Impact of Race, Rights, and Taxes on American Politics"*, authors Thomas and Mary Edsall refer to the present members of the Democratic Congress as "devoid of creative proposals and unwilling to act boldly." The Democratic Party has become the Conservative Party within the true meaning of the word conservative—resistant to change, unable or unwilling to try the NEW.

In the second chapter I listed chaos as the negative extreme of feminine Gender, and if there is any word that defines the present state of the Democratic Party it is chaotic. Like hens that runabout in every direction when the rooster is absent, the Democratic Party is running about in all different directions, without a philosophy, purpose or goal. How sad it is to receive their questionnaires when Presidential elections are in the offing, asking for help in preparing a platform, defining the issues, and setting an agenda. The Democratic Party has no idea as to what it should stand for. Is it any wonder then, that the powerful members of the party no longer choose to be involved in presidential politics? What real man would choose to identify himself with the chaos of the Democratic Party? Remember the days of Stevenson, Symington, Kefauver, Humphrey, Mansfield, Johnson, Connally, et al? They were powerful men who were willing to put their reputations on the line for what they believed in and for the glory of the Democratic Party. Who are the powerful members of that party today? Did you see their names on the ballot in New Hampshire?

The Democratic Party is impotent, sterile, a shadow of its former self, and it will meet the same fate of Eastern Europe, which collapsed because of the feminization of its economy. The Democratic Party will collapse because of the feminization of its body politic. It's over!

The Republican Party represents the masculine Gender in American politics, and within it there is the positive and negative manifestation of the masculine Gender. It believes in capitalism, of earning ones rewards, of justice, courage, and loyalty. It has not been known for its nurturing concerns, for its adaptability or willingness to negotiate. Whereas the Democratic Party represents the wife spending money for the nurturing of the race, the Republican Party represents the husband saying, "We can't afford any more." The Republican Party believes in fiscal responsibility, balanced budgets and efficiency. It fosters economic growth but is not very understanding of human frailty. Earlier in this century this party represented the extreme of the masculine Gender, fighting against any improvement in the lot of labor, the oppressed, the poor and the indigent. However, since the entire nation has taken a tilt towards the manifestations of the feminine Gender, it has tended to bring a balance to the philosophy of the party. The Republican Party is now considerably more mainstream than it used to be, or than the Democratic Party is at present.

This classification of mainstream, is really a more even balance of the manifestation of both Genders. It has little to do with clever politicking, master strategies, or the reapportionment of election districts. An example is the so called defection of the solid South from the Democratic to the Republican Party. The main social influences in the South are the respect for the military and religion. A disproportionate share of superior officers in the military still come from the South, and the South is still a very religiously oriented society. The military and religion are manifestations of the masculine Gender. Lest anyone take issue, spirituality has no Gender, but religion, which is essentially the governance of matters spiritual, is masculine in Gender. It was only natural that this masculine Gender oriented society would drift, and then run away from the extreme feminine Gender oriented Democratic Party.

It is also natural that the majority of people who voted for Patrick Buchanan were men. It is natural that David Duke is gaining in popularity with men. The issues are not race, religion, or even the avowedly conservative direction of these people. The issue is that chaos is at large in our land, and if something is not done about it we will self-destruct, as did Eastern Europe and as is happening to the Democratic Party. David Duke and Patrick Buchanan are saying something is fundamentally wrong in our nation, which is more than anyone else is saying. Perhaps they don't know what it is, but at least they know that something is wrong. The nation has veered to an extreme feminine Gender oriented thinking; that is the something that is wrong. Unless we come to that realization, and make appropriate corrections to our body politic, extremists and demagogues will come to the fore to take over our government.

As a nation, we have contented ourselves with an essentially feminine oriented domestic government and a masculine oriented national government, which is why we have a Democratic congress and a Republican executive branch. This combination is similar to that which men and women create in the marriage relationship. Within the home activities are primarily feminine Gender oriented, and outside of the home, matters tend to be primarily masculine Gender oriented. It is when this relationship evolves to an extreme in either direction, and sometimes in both directions, that troubles arise.

We have those two extremes in our government now, and as we approach the 21st century it should be obvious that America will be the Rome of that century, and these extremes should give us a sense of foreboding.

XXXIII
America - The Rome
of the 21st Century

Until the advent of the Gulf War, the world and we Americans had a perception of our military power as being strong, but containable. During the Gulf War, American military might was unveiled for all to see, and what was seen was a military machine of an awesome power beyond anything we had imagined.

No nation can be a threat to American military power for generations to come; therefore, we can continue to go about the world doing as we choose with impunity. We remove the president of Panama and try him in our own country, we invade Granada, bomb Libya, massacre Iraq, embargo Vietnam and Cuba, prop up the governments of the Philippines and Nicaragua, and tell the Japanese how to run their finances. We answer to no one, and expect that everyone will answer to us.

No matter that our SAT scores have dropped 25% and that Johnny can't read, count, or even speak very well, he certainly knows how to kill very well. The heinous decision of Allied War policy in World War II to kill as many civilians as possible led to the blanket bombing of German cities killing 250,000 civilians in a single night, and to the killing of equal numbers of Japanese civilians in the atomic bombings of Hiroshima and Nagasaki. We used napalm in Korea, agent orange in Vietnam, and cluster bombing in the Persian Gulf. During the Korean conflict General MacArthur suggested dropping atomic bombs on the five largest Chinese cities. The objective of these policies has always been the same, kill as many of everybody as possible.

This ruthlessness in warfare has been the norm of American military policy and was not limited to foreign activities, but was practiced on our brothers and sisters as well during the Civil War. The conditions in Andersonville prison in the South, and Johnson's Island in the North were as barbaric and inhumane as any treatment of prisoners in the annals of warfare.

Our tremendous military might, and our willingness to use it is what has made us the Rome of the 21st century. As Rome we are doing our utmost to ensure that other nations will remain powerless. It is natural for groupings of people, and for animals as well, to select leadership. With respect to the Arab world we have continually been against any nation that began to wear the badge of leadership. We were opposed to the United Arab Republic consisting of an alliance of Syria and Egypt, to Iran and Iraq. The dissolution of the Soviet Government will create a vacuum of leadership in Eastern Europe. The entire Mediterranean culture is now leaderless. In South America, we shore up weak governments and impede the progress of strong governments. This has been our policy in the Far East as well. It is natural for various nations to rise up and assume the role of leadership in a given area, but America will oppose these natural tendencies. So long as we prevent leadership, the flock will be ours to control. The American fleet sails in all waters and the American flag flies in all lands. We are the new Rome, and the world knows it.

The English historian, Thomas Macaulay said the following about our government: "Your Constitution is all sail and no anchor. Either some Caesar or Napoleon will seize the reins of government with a strong hand, or your republic will be laid waste by internal barbarians in the twentieth century as the Roman Empire was in the fifth." Recently the French government has expressed concern that America is sliding towards imperialism. As if to confirm these French fears, the following caption appeared on the front page of The

Wall Street Journal on February 2, 1992: "General Powell said he wants the world to be 'scared to death' of the U.S. military even after defense budget cuts, because that will comfort Washington's Allies and worry its enemies. The chairman of the Joint Chiefs of Staff stressed the need for a strong armed force and said his remarks weren't intended to be 'bellicose'." The world knows that we are on the way to becoming the Rome of the 21st century and our military has confirmed it.

How well do WE know it? Our military are all over the world, just as the Roman legions were, and our civilian life is also similar to that of Rome. Our gladiators perform in the various stadiums throughout the land, and were it not for modern medicine, many would be crippled for life. And some do die in the arena. It is no longer necessary to take a tour of Rome to learn debauchery from the ancients; these things can be seen on most any newsstand in America. Rome was a government of an aristocratic oligarchy-a government of the few-and we are gravitating towards such a government. Jesus told us to render unto Caesar that which is Caesar's; however, we expect Caesar to be responsible for our economy, education, safety and morals. Soon we will be rendering unto Caesar everything.

And we shall have our Caesars.

We have desecrated the American flag, ridiculed the national anthem, and shown increasing disdain and disrespect for those in office. "Hail Caesar, we are preparing the way for you."

The choices that remain open to us are what kind of Rome we shall be, and the kind of Caesars that shall represent us. The reason that we will have a Caesar is because the men of this nation failed to use their natural rulership ability early in this century and instead opted to become full-fledged wage earners. They became jackasses on the treadmill of production instead of exercising leadership in the administration of the family, tribe and race. The women of this nation, not being equipped to rule, and wanting to emulate the men, also got on the treadmill of production. We have become a nation of jackasses and she-asses on the treadmill of production, each sex forfeiting the positive manifestations of their respective Genders, and their responsibilities to the family, tribe and race. There can only be one kind of Caesar to rule in such a situation, a Caesar who rules by decree in a Rome of followers.

If we want a better Rome and a better Caesar, then we must take control of our lives; assume our responsibilities and obligations to one another, to the family, tribe and race. We must have spiritually based values, a desire to propagate and preserve the species, a respect for the differences in Gender, and an economic system independent of the State.

The few remaining chapters will be devoted to our relationship with one another and steps to be taken for a better society.

XXXIV
The Task at Hand

There was a time when men left the tribe in search of new hunting areas, or to do combat with an enemy, the women stayed behind and attended to the means of production and the nurturing of the tribe. One of these activities was milking the cows, which was done by hand. Some of this milk was then churned by hand into butter. Machines were invented that could automatically milk the cows and other machines were invented that would churn the butter. Eventually machines replaced the milkmaid, and women associated with the production of milk and butter became dairy owners and operators. The only change that occurred in this short story was the production of milk and butter. Women did not change!

There was a time when as men looked for new hunting and farming areas for the growing needs of an expanding tribe, they would climb mountains to see what was on the other side. Sometimes they were away for weeks, as they traveled on foot and there were no roads or paths. With the domestication of the horse, they were able to travel greater distances in less time. With the advent of the automobile, and then the plane, scouting the terrain was accomplished in a matter of hours. The only change that occurred in this short story was the means of getting to the other side of the mountain. Men did not change!

The fundamental nature of the sexes, and their requirements of and contribution to the family, tribe and race has not changed; he means of serving the family, tribe and race have changed. That is all. The fundamental nature of Gender in the universe has not, cannot, and will not change.

However, the natural manifestation of Gender has been misdirected. With the advent of the second Industrial Revolution, men left their homes to earn money with which to clothe and feed their families. Men had always pioneered and created for the benefit of the family, race, and tribe; and this movement out of the home was initially a means of pioneering and creating in order to continue supplying these benefits. However, this activity of earning became all consuming, and men neglected their governing function with respect to the family, tribe, and race. At first, the effects on society were almost imperceptible because of the strong ethnic and religious traditions that maintained a tribal order and stability. However, with the intermixing of various ethnic and religious cultures, society became increasingly ordered by government, rather than by cultural tradition. Since men were not at home for much more than eating and sleeping, the task of governance fell upon women. This was a task for which they were not suited and therefore resulted in dire consequences.

The natural manifestation of the feminine Gender has always been nurturing and producing. Women produce what men create and use the results of this production to nurture the race. However, left to their own resources they will nurture indiscriminately. The excess on the positive side of this misdirected nurturing will be exhaustion. The excess on the negative side will be self-aggrandizement and narcissism.

The nurturing manifestation of the last half of this century can be seen everywhere. We have buses designed to pick up wheel chairs and to tip towards the infirm pedestrian to assist in their boarding. We have sloped sidewalks to accommodate those who use motorized wheelchairs. The entire movement of environmentalism is a feminine Gender manifestation, whether for cleaner air or water, or protection of endangered species, the limitation of pesticides, the control of atomic waste, the purity of our food, or noise reduction. The expanding practice of holistic medicine, natural childbirth, and nutritional concerns are all manifestations of the nurturing aspect of feminine Gender.

Yet with all these positive nurturing activities, why is it that we have more than one million men in jail, and promises to put even more in jail? Why are children living in the streets? Why are children being born with substance abuse addictions? Why are we becoming increasingly security conscious, buying all sorts of defensive weapons and security systems? Why can't Johnny read? Why is there such a high incidence of rape? Why are we becoming polarized by income, ethnicity, race, religion, and occupation? Why are we litigating against each other with increasing frequency? Why is trust towards others and towards institutions decreasing? Why are women's bodies rotting away from substance abuse and venereal disease? Why are there more and more people afraid to make the commitment of marriage? Why have we lost confidence in our government? Why can we no longer live with our parents, our children, our brothers and sisters? Why do mothers and daughters resent each other? Why are fathers and sons at war with each other? Why are we more concerned with getting even than with justice? Why are we spending vast sums of time and money in attempts to avoid the propagation and preservation of humankind? Why is this all happening if we are living in an era of tremendous nurturing?

Why is there more publicity and media attention given to the protection of the dolphin than to the protection of our young? Why are we more concerned about the abuse of calves that are raised for veal, than we are about our brothers in prison who frequently are living in worse conditions? Why the national clamor over the preservation of the spotted owl, when our children are being shot in schoolrooms? Why are we more concerned with the caribou on the north slope of Alaska, than we are about our children who are suffering from malnutrition? Why are we so concerned about the endangered species of animal life, when the sacred species of women and children are endangered?

The nurturing manifestation is indeed misdirected, or to be more precise, the nurturing manifestation is indiscriminate, and requires the presence of the masculine Gender to give it direction. Also, mother's milk flows most freely and abundantly when she is protected and feels secure, a feeling that does not apply to most women today. After the lion staked out the territory, the lioness knew she had a secure place in which to hunt and raise her cubs. She was able to do her nurturing well in the knowledge that she was protected. Security, confidence, trust, and appreciation, are the arenas in which the feminine Gender is most productive and nurturing; only the active manifestation of the masculine Gender can provide these conditions.

However, when the positive aspects of masculine Gender are missing, the nurturing ability of the feminine Gender is weakened, and what nurturing is available is misdirected. As this century draws to a close we are witnessing the cumulative impact of the influence of the tyrant mother and absent father that began early in this century. We have men and women who no longer know their function or purpose for being. We have women who have been hurt severely in their childhood and are unable to give of themselves for fear of being hurt again. Instead of nurturing men they nurture cats, dogs, parakeets and goldfish. On a subconscious level they only go out with men whom they know they will not love, for this offers their hearts protection—it also deprives them of joy. We have men who are unable to drop their defenses and allow women to get close enough to love and nurture them. We have a society of men who have given up their every natural masculine function to the State, and have become the modern-day slaves. They have gone even further, and legislated away their innate powers as men, in what is surely an act of self-immolation. And the women have done likewise, seeking out and associating with men who abuse them, indeed looking for this abuse, replicating their abused childhoods and atoning for the resultant anger. We have become a nation of weak anodes and ineffective cathodes, with the electricity of life reduced to a trickle.

The task at hand is to restore the balance of Gender to our lives so that we may properly care for the family, tribe and race. We need desperately to be nurtured, all of us. We need desperately to feel secure, all of us. Only then will we be able to provide the leadership, direction, creativity, nurturing that will lead to the mental, physical, and emotional well being of the race.

I have stated frequently that the weakening of the manifestation of the masculine Gender began early in this century. In the March 9, 1992 issue of TIME in which Gloria Steinem was interviewed, she stated that the 20th century was a feminist century. It was! That is probably the only statement that the Queen of American Feminism and I will agree on. It should be noted, that in the eight-page spread on Feminism contained in TIME, the family, tribe, and race were not mentioned. The men in prison, the children being shot on the streets and in schools, were not mentioned, The addicted mothers, the homeless, the uneducated were not mentioned. Mentioned instead was the narcissistic self; the self-aggrandized, self-centered, lesbian-promoting, and man-hating philosophy of the sick few.

In mentioning the feminists here, I do want to imply that they are the problem that the task at hand needs to correct. They are merely the extreme manifestation of the underlying problem. They are she flies sucking on the blood of a hemorrhaging nation. They need to be flicked away so that the wounds can be tendered. Once the wounds are healed, they will have nothing to suck on, and will disappear.

In discussing this book with a politically active woman, she indicated that while she disagreed with a lot of what I had to say, there was also a lot that she could agree with, but that I should not expect the men to take any action. She said that men discuss their jobs, make a little locker room talk, and that is the extent of their social involvement. She said that if I expected to make any societal changes, I would have to enlist the support of the women. I had come to that conclusion many years earlier, but it did disturb me to hear it from someone else, whether man or woman.

Therein lies the real challenge—to have men be interested in more than their jobs and occasional locker room talk, and to be motivated to societal action. After more than a century of being hooked to the machinery of production, men have come to view themselves as just wage earners, and indeed, have become just that.

They have forgotten that the means of production that they have attached themselves to are the result of the pioneering spirit and creative Will of the masculine Gender. Men have become the slaves of their own creation. Being chained to the machinery of production is not the natural place for man to be. Man's purpose is to pioneer, create and govern.

A bright ray of hope that men will wake up and realize and start exercising their responsibilities came from the picture *"Boyz N the Hood"*, in which the writer/director John Singleton does not imply, but comes right out and states that fathers are needed to raise boys to be men. These fathers are needed even though the boys might have highly credentialized mothers.

It is my belief that those who are graduating from college now are the forerunners of a generation who will bring about significant social change. Unlike their brothers and sisters of the sixties and seventies who tore down institutions, these youth will build up institutions. They will develop new forms of government, new forms of the economy, and new forms of worship. If there is any hope that the Rome of the 21st century can be a just and benevolent one, it will come from the efforts of this generation.

A seemingly unlikely source that is helping men to be freed from the chains of production is the Women's Movement. As women pour into the labor force, more and more men are being released from the productive process. The men do not realize this as a benefit yet, instead they look upon it as contributing to their difficulty in obtaining employment, or causing their unemployment. But this movement of women putting proportionately more time in the labor force, and men putting proportionately less time, will bring about a more natural balance of the influence of Gender.

As men became engrossed in, dedicated to, and enslaved by, the means of production, they "left to the women" the societal functions naturally attended to by men. Since women are not naturally equipped to handle these functions, the government assumed a greater and greater roll in the administration of the activities of the family and tribe. The government now deals with teenage pregnancy, unwed motherhood, scholastic standards, the care of the aged and the training of the young, the disciplining of adolescent boys, crime, litter, and health. As has been indicated in many chapters of this letter, the governments handling of these matters has been a dismal failure. Consequently society is living in fear, apprehension and distrust.

And still the men do nothing.

We buy burglar alarms for our cars and homes. we put shields between the personnel of post offices and banks, and the customers whom they serve. Women travel with mace in their purses, learn to use hand guns, and take martial arts courses.

And still the men do nothing.

Teenage pregnancy is on the increase, high schools are now dispensers of condoms instead of centers of education, and malnutrition is rampant among our infants.

And still the men do nothing.

The men are so inured to their status as wage earners that they do not understand, and consequently do not exercise their innate ability to govern. Even the highly educated, who put in 80 hour weeks on Wall street, in law firms, in accounting firms, as physicians and surgeons in hospitals, no longer exercise their manly ability to govern. The more money they earn, the more they spend on security and on escaping from their issue-laden environment.

However, there is no escape-only a temporary avoidance. The issues must be dealt with. And those who realize that it is their obligation to deal with these issues and who have the courage to deal with these issues, are called men. The rest, well, call them what you will-wimps, weak-kneed milksops, peanut butter cookies-certainly not protectors of the family, tribe and race.

The task at hand then is to get the men to do something. And to accomplish this the women must do their part. Their part will be to tell the men to "do something". When you women read of the increased incidence of crime say "do something" to your man. When you hear that Johnny can't read say "do something." When you see that the economy is down, say, "Do something." Get him off the sofa, out of the easy chair and into the arena. Say, "Do something."

The next chapter will deal with the action to be taken—once men decide to "do something."

XXXV
The Action Required

The masculine influence must be returned to the family structure, and the starting point is for fathers to return home. This especially pertains to those fathers who have been enticed out of, or kicked out of, their homes in order for the mothers to be recipients of welfare. To those men I say, "Go home". Do not concern yourselves with changing the law; that will come in time. This book is not about the law; it is about improving the lot of society now. For those of you who have left because of reasons other than the law—go home. Your wife, your woman, and your children need you. Go home!

You men who are putting in 80-hour work weeks, cut down, and spend some time at home. Who are you working for and for what ends? Be with those for whom you toil, and witness their joy at your presence. Go home!

Devote some of the extra hours away from the job to the community. Get involved with the zoning board, the school board, the parks department, and the multitudinous opportunities for volunteerism. Maintain relations with the police and support them in their efforts to protect the family and tribe. Let the masculine presence be felt and respected in the community. There is nothing in the governance of the tribe that should be "left to the women." They are doing more than you in the nurturing of the race, and expect that you will make the community a safe nest. Walk the streets of your community, and speak to all the people; the shopkeepers, the newsstand operator, the beggar, the homeless, the bank teller, the postal clerk, the trash collector. For those who live in apartment houses, condominiums, co-ops, at least get to know everyone on your floor, and by name. You are in this world, know your brothers and sisters who inhabit it with you.

There must be a return to a tribal way of life. The new tribe must be based on geography, on community, not on the old and disappearing foundations of ethnicity, race or religion. We should have floor captains, or leaders, or representatives in each multi apartment building. We must participate in more involved block associations. These activities should be required of all men, regardless of economic or educational station.

We must become substantially more involved in the institutions that educate our youth, the majority of which have become coeducational. The rational of this coed education has been that it will cause the different sexes to relate better, inasmuch as the sexes are intermingling more at the workplace and elsewhere. It appears that coeducational instruction has been successful in attaining that objective. However, if the primary objective of education is to impart academic knowledge, then coeducational instruction has been a dismal failure. In single sex schools, girls and women do better at subjects that are considered to be male oriented, than they do when taking these same subjects in coeducational institutions. Boys and men do better at activities that are considered to be feminine oriented, when in single sex schools than when in coeducational institutions. For a detailed scholarly and objective review of this matter, a report is available prepared by Professor David Riesman of Harvard University. The facts are that the average SAT scores have dropped 25% in the past decade. From a practical viewpoint, men can not create and invent if they can not read, write and count. In passing, it should also be noted that at some educational institutions 25% of the women have been sexually molested. This is hardly an indication of good relationships between the sexes.

Our youth must be counseled, guided and cared for, especially those males attaining puberty, whose energies need directing and disciplining. Recreational areas must be provided, with supervision but with a minimum of involvement. The boys must be left to deal with the relationship of their peer group under the watchful eye of a masculine presence. Activities such as those provided by the Police Athletic League and YMCA must be increased, and Little League everything must be decreased.

Our youth must be taught honor, truthfulness, responsibility, courage, steadfastness, and an expanded sense of comradery.

Young men must be motivated to get married. Married men produce 50% more than single men do, are aware of the elderly, the training of the young and the responsibilities towards the family and tribe. Single men earn enough to take care of their entertainment and to occasionally have something soft and smooth alongside of them. Marriage is a high order of tribal responsibility, surpassed only by parenthood, both of which should be given the proper place in society. The exceptions are the priesthood and some aspects of the military. To be a man is to realize one's responsibility towards the family, tribe and race.

Our streets, parks, playgrounds, and other public places must be made safe. Children should be able to play without fear of molestation or abduction, women should be able to walk the streets without fear of mugging, and use the parks without fear of rape. Protection of women and children is a primary responsibility of men, and it is time that this responsibility is exercised.

An appreciation of the nature of the opposite sex must be inculcated in all youth, and an understanding of the responsibilities to one another must be developed.

Designations of ethnicity, race, and religious orientation must be eliminated from all governmental rules, regulations, statues, and ordinances. Ethnicity stems from geographical boundaries, race stems from climatic locations, religion stems from the needs of God's children at a particular place and time. There is but one race and that is the human race, there is but one ethnicity in this nation and that is American, there is but one God and many perceptions. To address a man as other than your brother is to profess your own ignorance. For the law to address a man with a designation other than that of man is to regard him as inferior, a classification that can only produce negative results.

The conditions that foster creativity must be reestablished, for this nation is dangerously short of new products, especially those of a conceptual nature. The creative Will is a manifestation of the masculine Gender, and it has been stifled in the last half of this century. The motivation has decreased because of the decrease in the percentage of married men, the ability has decreased because of the failure of our educational institutions, the opportunities have decreased because of an equalization of the sexes in the workplace by government decree, the means have decreased by siphoning money away from small business and channeling it into big business and governmental activities, neither of which make for economic growth.

There are one million men in jail, and more in line to get in. Some of these men must be released from prison. The conditions are inhuman. Their incarceration is conditioning them to become hardened criminals. They are being deprived of the multi-faceted benefits of associating with the feminine Gender, and it shows. Men become brutes when removed for extended periods from the presence of women. The penal system must be changed. Public humiliation, forgiveness and a chance at rehabilitation are much more effective than hiding the law-breakers from us and treating them worse than dogs.

We must deal with those lonely, frightened, and neglected youths, who are members of street gangs, and give them direction, love, understanding and the discipline necessary to lead productive lives.

We must legalize the use of drugs, which will break the drug cartel, reduce the power of government, and eliminate drug pushers.

We must improve the health of our environment and the quality of our infrastructure. We must find ways of caring for the needs of an ever-growing population. We must prepare for extensive space activities, for the universe is our domain, and we must explore it.

We must reestablish a sense of morality in our laws. The first amendment is not scripture. It is merely part of the laws created by a group of men who formed a new government and who were disappointed with this government not long after it was created. The first amendment was not intended to give free license for any form of conduct, but was intended to provide freedom of speech "within" the moral framework of the time. Sacred writings come from the Torah, the Bible, the Koran, the Upanishads, the Bhagavad-Gita, the Tao, and the teachings of Confucius and the Buddha. The moral standards of any time are what the average of the populace can readily adhere to. There must be morality in all that we do.

The high incidence of teenage pregnancy is not correctable by the dispersing of condoms by the state; it is correctable by fathers who are at home and who do not trust the boys and men their daughters go out with.

Unwed motherhood and the deleterious effect that it has on the offspring must be curtailed. Being a single parent must be shown for what it is, a means whereby children are denied the benefit of a balanced Gender influence in their lives.

All this and more must be accomplished. It requires determination and courage. It requires the Will to serve our brothers and sisters.

What will your sisters think of these proposals? If there are one million men in jail, that means there are almost one million mothers who lay awake in bed at night grieving for their sons. What will they think of you if you get their sons out of prison? There are one million youth involved in street gangs, and who shoot at and kill each other by the tens of thousands each year. What will their mothers think of you if you bring this madness to a halt? There are millions of children whose academic performance is decreasing. What will their mothers think of you if their children develop an appreciation of learning and inspired academic performance? What will women say if they can once again walk the streets in relative safety? You will have more than just support from the women, they will throw flowers at your feet and place garlands on your head. Do not be concerned with the radicals who, after the initial bra burning will be laughed out of society. We are talking serious matters here, matters of living or dying. Wake up my brothers and see the task at hand and the action to be taken. Be men and do what is required and expected of you. The women will be grateful and will support you.

XXXVI
Our Nurturing
Requirements

The call to action in this book has been directed at men, for as has been expounded in every chapter, the ills of society are a result of the lack of masculine involvement.

This does not mean that the manifestation of the feminine Gender is irrelevant. Quite to the contrary, and as has also been expounded, there must be a balance of Gender influence in society. However, there is no lack of the manifestation of the feminine Gender in society today, although it is severely misdirected, and frequently the negative aspects are being fostered.

Only rarely are the positive aspects of the feminine Gender promulgated. Too often we hear "Is that all that you do?", or "don't you work?", or "she doesn't do anything", when referring to a woman who has a husband and children, but no outside employment. This "party line" has become so pervasive that women are becoming increasingly intimidated about expressing their inherent strength and natural inclinations. So now they say of themselves, "We don't 'just' nurture," "I don't 'only' take care of my family", "I do 'more' than take care of the house". Or, to get deeper into the ideology of the "party line," "I need self-fulfillment," or "Now I'm doing something that lets me 'express' myself". All these statements infer that wife and mother are on the low level of recognition and respect by society, and that nurturing is neither self-fulfilling nor self-expressing. Let us look into these three categories: just, only and more; self-fulfillment and self-expression; and recognition and respect in more detail.

"Just", "only", and "more" are references made regarding the nurturing function of womanhood. Yet, is there anything in all existence that is needed more than nurturing? When life is young the nurturing requirement is obvious, whether it be infants, kittens, or puppies, but as life matures, the need to be nurtured continues, and food is not the only nourishment needed. Other nurturing requirements are tenderness, compassion, encouragement and attention. The masculine Gender attributes of fairness, justice, honor and steadfastness, do not provide the nurturing needed, they merely help to secure an environment conducive to nurturing. Nurturing is the great need of all existence. We pray to God for spiritual nourishment, look to the sun for the energy that will enable the earth to provide our material nourishment, and look to our women for psychological nourishment.

This need to be nurtured permeates all existence, and the desire to nurture is an expression of love, the very fuel of existence. It is this quality of the feminine Gender that motivates the masculine Gender to accomplishment. Contrary to the perverse philosophy of the "party line" it is not what is between a woman's legs that motivates men to climb mountains, navigate the oceans and cross deserts. It is not what is between a woman's legs that makes a man endure hardship, work in almost intolerable conditions, and devote his life to his wife and family. No, it is never that good. What motivates a man comes from the heart of a woman, and every man needs that which flows from her heart. Every man wants to bask in the aura of a giving, nurturing woman. Every man, and every child—male or female, needs the nurturing warmth that exudes from the presence of a loving woman. The depiction of supermen such as Hank Reardon in the novel *"Atlas Shrugged"* is a romantic fantasy. Successful, powerful, sensitive men, all have a woman or women, alongside or around them. Powerful men who do not have a woman in their lives become ruthless. Children who do not have nurturing in their lives develop a painful emptiness that can lead to an overpowering loneliness. Nurturing is not a "just" or "only" function; it is the warmth of the universe.

However, the race is hurting because of its lack of nurturing. Articles and books are being written with increasing frequency about the lack of nurturing being suffered by our youth. The latest of these is a book by David Hamburg entitled *"Today's Children: Creating a Future for a Generation in Crisis."* Mr. Hamburg is president of the Carnegie Corporation and says that the U.S. is committing atrocities on its children and that we have already lost a substantial portion of the generation of children under age 16. These children need to be nurtured, and they can not be nurtured in absentia. "Quality time" regarding the nurturing of children comes from the "party line" and is a myth. Quality time applies to the masculine influence in the home or community. Discipline can be established and respect for mother inculcated in a very short time, leaving men free to go about the business of obtaining the material substance for nurturing, whether it be finding new lands, or inventing new products. It gives men time to see that the nest is protected and that the enemy will make no incursions. The time that fathers are at home can be quality time. But the requirements of nurturing are continuous. We eat every day and we breathe every minute. The nurturing requirement is not sporadic, it is constant. As a "Peanuts" cartoon once indicated, "security is—opening the front door and hearing mom in the kitchen." If this is the criterion for security, which in this illustration means nurturing, then there are many children who are insecure. If there is any doubt, ask the children which they prefer, coming home to a house with mom in the kitchen or coming home to an empty house. Men too, like coming home to a house with their wives in the kitchen. In fact, the reason that a man comes to the house is because of the nurturing that a woman puts inside of it. Men in prison, children in detention centers and in orphanages, also need nurturing. Children who are sent to day care centers, nursery schools, and all day baby sitters, need to be nurtured. The race needs to be nurtured, and this nurturing is not a "just" or "only" function for those who provide it, or for those who receive it. It is an integral and necessary part of existence, and those who do not receive it, and there are many, are starving just as badly as those who have no bread to eat.

Is this function of nurturing not self-fulfilling and self-expressing? Before you answer this my sisters, I ask you another question. Have you ever seen a bachelor pad? Not the apartment of a divorced man who has half the furnishings that his wife purchased during their marriage, or that of a young man whose mother helped him furnish it, but have you seen a bachelor's apartment that he himself furnished? The words austere and sparse only begin to describe it. Barren and primitive are more appropriate descriptions. Did you marry a man who had an apartment such as that? Did you get him to move to a larger apartment and furnish it with curtains, rugs, mirrors, knickknacks, furniture, china, glassware and other accouterments that were absent from his bachelor pad? Every man lives in the home his wife makes for him and has the social life that his wife creates for him. Have you made a home and created a social life for a man? Have you brought life into this world and nurtured it? Have you seen your offspring grow from helpless infants to self-sufficient adulthood? Now answer the question that started this paragraph.

Can a woman provide this nurturing activity without a husband or a child, or in addition to having a husband and a child? Of course she can. She can perform the nurturing act as a schoolteacher, surgeon, subway token taker, retail storeowner, attorney or cab driver. Those women who nurture as they work are a joy to deal with, and also most likely enjoy the work that they do. Also, various changes in technology and marketing allow women to be with their families when needed, and do their employment activities when not needed by the family. The use of the computer enables many functions to be done at home that used to require the use of an office. Direct marketing allows women to work hours that do not interfere with their family obligations. In the case of factory work, the trend will be to have child-care, nurseries and playgrounds at the jobsite.

However, in the case of married women with children, why should the family be sacrificed for outside activity, whether work or entertainment? Single parents of course do not have that option, but unless the trend of single parenthood is reversed, the devastation wrought upon our children will not be reversible.

Who says that nurturing is not worthy of recognition or respect? The children? The men? The women who are doing the nurturing?

People who say that nurturing is an insufficient activity for women are those who cannot do it; those who have failed; whose concept of life is self serving and narcissistic at best, and filled with anger and resentment at worst, and care not one iota for the family, tribe, and race. Self-serving and lecherous women who brag about how many lovers they had, whether heterosexual, bisexual, or lesbian-those who do not know what it is to have a real man at home-will not hold nurturing in high regard. And finally, those whose lives are so distraught that a lifetime of therapy won't cure them will not hold nurturing in high regard. Do you think you will benefit from the views of these people?

Isn't it natural to consult with those who have experienced what we have, and succeeded at it? Do we not normally emulate those who succeed rather than those who fail? In a recent New York lecture Faith Popcorn, author of *"The Popcorn Report"* and current marketing guru, said that the woman of the 1990's is Barbara Bush. By this she meant that Mrs. Bush is representative of the symbol of American womanhood for the remainder of this century. I feel that Mrs. Schwarzkopf is another representative of that symbol. These women raised and nurtured a family. They were loyal to powerful husbands whose professions made high demands of their time and presence. They earned their stripes, medals, and love and admiration of their husbands. Their husbands know that they couldn't be where they are today without the support their wives had given them. They are neither svelte or chick, but they have fine minds and exude nurturing. I do hope that Faith Popcorn is right, and that these women and others who have done as much, will be the symbols of American womanhood for the balance of this decade. They are positive symbols. They are moving the race forward.

XXXVII
Portnoy and
the Boyz

The novel *"Portnoy's Complaint"* described the absent or unassertive father and the resultant Tyrant Mother. It was written from the Jewish perspective because the writer was a Jew, but the conditions written about permeated our nation.

The film *"Boyz and the Hood"* portrays a society in which there is little parental guidance given to children. Fathers are not at home and the mothers can't cope. It was written from the black perspective because the writer was black, but the conditions written about permeate our nation.

The conditions written about in Portnoy and Boyz were no more unique to a tribal grouping than were the conditions written about in *"Studs Lonnegan"*. The author of "Studs," James Farrel, was Irish and he wrote from the Irish perspective, but what he wrote about was not unique to the Irish. Poverty, the breakdown of the tribal structure, and the resultant aimlessness, resignation, and hopelessness of the depression era were symptomatic of our nation at that time.

In a fish tank, whatever happens to one fish, influences all the fish, and whatever one fish does, influences all the fish. There is no way in which to care for one fish or one group of fish, at the exclusion of the others. Our nation can be perceived as one huge fish bowl with various shapes and colors of fish, and whatever one of us does affects the rest, and whatever the rest do, affects us. There can be no "them" and "us" in a fish tank. We are all in it together. However when people think in terms of "them" and "us", is when governments fall. The conditions that Philip Roth, James Farrel and John Singleton wrote about affected or are still affecting all of us. The remedies for these conditions are dependent upon the active involvement of all of us.

John Singleton must be an extremely perceptive young man to have at the age of twenty-two recognized and been able to portray the inner hurt, turmoil, anger, helplessness, tension, frustration and loneliness of people. In the last scene of Boyz, when Doughboy tells Trey that he has no brother, that he has no mother, he was expressing the empty and lonely feeling of millions of men who either never had a mother, or were disowned by their mother, or whose mother preferred another offspring, and/or who have no wives or women friends that love them. Having a gun and being tough didn't make up for the lack of nurturing in his life. The film indicates that Doughboy dies two weeks later, but actually Doughboy was dead already, he was just doing time until his soul left the earth.

Doughboy's mother, while favoring his step brother, portrayed the anxiety of a mother hoping for the best for her son, wanting to see him succeed, unable to cope with the violence of the neighborhood or the discipline required of teenagers. She gave birth to two sons, raised them, only to see both of them murdered in their teens. Her anxiety is the anxiety all mothers have when their children are in danger, her agony is the agony of all mothers who lose their children. Her frustration is the frustration of all mothers who do not have a man at home.

For those who feel that Boyz does not represent the world in which they live, I suggest you take off your intellectual blinders, your perceptive restraints, and take steps to treat your awareness for myopia. For those in the cities, do you not hear the car alarms going off all night, the sirens of police cars and ambulances? Do you not see the steel gates over retail store windows, the plastic protection in banks and post offices, and the ever-increasing building security?

Those in small towns, are you not aware of the drugs being dealt, the rapes that are occurring? The Hood is not just in Los Angeles, Chicago and New York. The Hood is everywhere in America. The Hood is America today.

I consider *Portnoy's Complaint* and *Boyz N the Hood* to be the Alpha and Omega of the change in the balance of the manifestation of Gender in twentieth century America. Portnoy indicated the seeds that had been sown, but little attention had been paid by society. Boyz indicates the harvest of what was sown. I hope that we will all realize what has been reaped, and that we will all do our part to plant a different crop.

XXXVIII
A Time for
Renewed Courage

As American automobile plants were being closed, and the President went to Japan with the automobile executives, the women cried because of their loss of jobs, the men cried, the union cried, Lee Iacocca cried, and the President vomited.

Two of the above events were natural: the women crying and the President vomiting. The other events were a disgrace and illustrative of the decline in the manifestation of the masculine Gender.

When a woman's nest is in jeopardy it is a natural response for her to be anxious. It is also natural for her to expect a man to "do something" to correct the situation or alleviate the effects. She does not expect a man to stand there and cry with her. If a man no longer feels that it is his responsibility to find alternatives, or that he has the ability to do so, then who else should? The government? If so, then we are indeed ready for Caesar. Then we are a nation of sheep waiting for the government to find and feed us.

As for the unions, they still have not learned that new products and services, and new companies, are what in turn create a demand for their services. Instead, they call upon governments to support businesses that are dying or becoming obsolete. What would have happened to our economy had there been strong unions for the kerosene lamp makers, the buggy whip makers, and the wagon wheel makers?

The heads of the large corporations, exemplified by Mr. Iacocca, are also incapable of promoting economic growth. Large corporations rarely create or pioneer—they administer. And their quest for government support is similar to that of the unions and the workers.

While the workers, the unions, and the corporations espouse free enterprise, the fact is they are all crying for government support. They have all lost the pioneering risk taking manifestation of the masculine Gender. Small wonder that the President regurgitated. He was truly representing those red-blooded men and women who are left in this country with some semblance of guts. That whole picture of crying workers, and crying unions, and crying companies symbolized by a crying Mr. Iacocca, was sickening.

This is not to say that losing one's source of income is not a devastating experience, and that the situation must be addressed. As I write this book I can speak first hand of the demoralizing effect of financial hardship. I am 62 years old, divorced, unemployed and without benefits, without possessions, living on credit cards, and can only last another two or three months without finding some alternative income source. Nevertheless, I realize that my road back to financial success is, or should be, dependent upon the person that I see in the mirror, not the person in Washington.

This is true for all of us, and to the degree that we recognize this truth, and "do something" about it, we will once again take control of lives, become financially secure and create a better environment in which to live.

Our country did not always have automobile assembly plants; men of vision and courage who risked everything they owned to bring their dreams to reality created them. We must realize that even before the assembly plants, the people who developed our land were pioneers who experienced hardship and faced complete financial loss. This nation was built by men and women who were willing to gamble their last dollar, who were willing to endure brutal environmental conditions, who worked long hours, and who were willing to chance the unknown. These people experienced fear and trepidation, but they had the courage to push on.

Shall we have the courage to start anew? Or shall we be as the prisoner who when set free, asked to be allowed back in prison because he was unable to make his way in the world? Shall we be as a slave who when given his freedom, asked to be taken back by his master because he could not sustain himself. Are we begging to be re-hooked to the assembly line because we cannot exist without it? Have we decided to become slaves to the industrial machine? Are we crying because our masters have set us free? In the book of Genesis the following directive is given: "Be fruitful and increase, fill the earth and subdue it, rule over the fish of the sea, the birds of heaven, and every living thing that moves upon the earth." Having been given this directive, can we not at least control our own lives?

This is a time for courage. Courage to reassert ourselves and take control of our lives and give it direction. Courage to buck the "party line." Courage to be a man and be proud of it. Courage to be a woman and proud of it. Courage to realize that the differences in Gender supplement each other, instead of complimenting each other. Courage to make sure that the economy and government are vehicles for the preservation and propagation of the race, not ends unto themselves. Courage to live the lives we were put on this earth to live. Courage to live out the belief that every man is our brother and every woman our sister.

If this book has reached you, if you recognize the issues at hand and the action necessary to correct these issues, then act. Have the courage to act my brothers and sisters. You have two options and one choice. One option is that the State will have responsibility for every aspect of our lives. The other option is that we will have responsibility for every aspect of our lives. There is but one choice. Choose well.

Printed in the United States
69513LVS00002BA/3